GOALS AND SETTING GOALS

Goals and Setting Goals

Children dream of great but improbable futures. Some want to be a national leader, a movie star or a great sportsman. When children grow into adults, most learn there's a difference between the dreams of childhood and realistic goals.

A well-defined goal is realistic and achievable. An achievable goal is a tool to help you reach your destination. There are several benefits to defining achievable goals.

In some science fiction novels and movies, the future of work is bleak. Work in the future is often portrayed as dull, repetitive, and dehumanizing.

Opportunities for change, challenge, and growth make work and life more interesting and fulfilling. When writers and moviemakers want to depict a dreary future, they describe a future without these opportunities.

Why do people so often fail to keep their New Year's resolutions? Many times it's because they've set goals for themselves that can't be achieved.

Achievable goals have two required components: an objective component and a standards component. A third optional component--a conditions component--may also be included to support the required components.

There's more to setting a goal than simply choosing a destination you want to reach. Setting goals requires strategic thinking to help you anticipate obstacles and collaboration with people who can help you overcome those obstacles.

When you practice strategic thinking as you set goals, you gain several important benefits.

A majority of your work-related goals require participation from others in your organization. Strategic thinking helps you identify people who can help you achieve your goals so you can gain their cooperation.

The purpose of setting a goal is to gain a reward. However, striving for a goal means you must also accept the risk of failure.

Setting any work-related goal requires an investment of time and effort. If you attain your goal, your investment results in success. However, there's always a risk you'll fail to achieve a goal and your time and effort will be lost.

The amount of risk in a goal correlates to the time and effort required to achieve it. Low-risk goals usually require a small amount of investment of time and effort. High-risk goals often require a large investment of time and effort.

Some goals may seem too hard to achieve on your own.

When you need help to achieve a goal, that's a good time to find a partner with whom you can collaborate.

The people who can help you achieve your goals won't always share your goals. Their goals may even conflict with yours. You can resolve conflicts and build partnerships by applying these steps to create a collaborative goal:

- Define the conflict.
- Propose a collaboration.
- Define collaborative roles.

There's a big difference between a goal and an accomplishment. Setting a goal is the beginning of a process. If you're successful, an accomplishment comes at the end of the process.

Few people enjoy the luxury of pursuing only one goal at a time. Most have to juggle several goals simultaneously.

When you pursue several goals at once, you have to prioritize some goals ahead of others. There are two elements that determine the priority you assign to any goal:

- the importance or value of achieving the goal,
- the availability of resources needed to reach the goal.

There will be times when you can't achieve some of your goals. That's when it's time to consider alternative goals.

ACHIEVABLE GOALS

Achievable goals

Children dream of great but improbable futures. Some want to be a national leader, a movie star or a great sportsman. When children grow into adults, most learn there's a difference between the dreams of childhood and realistic goals.

A well-defined goal is realistic and achievable. An achievable goal is a tool to help you reach your destination. There are several benefits to defining achievable goals.

First, an achievable goal organizes and guides your work-related decisions and activities. When you strive for a clearly defined, achievable goal, you pursue decisions and activities that help you make progress in reaching that goal.

Second, achievable goals give you a way to monitor your personal progress.

As you draw nearer to reaching a goal, you can see how far you've come and how far you still have to go. You can see for yourself how much progress you've made.

Finally, goals give you a basis for communicating with others about how you perform your job.

See each type of goal to learn more about it.

Professional goals

When you talk about your professional goals, you're telling others how you plan to do your job or what you've accomplished.

Personal goals

When you discuss your personal goals, you're explaining what's important to you and how you're working to change yourself.

Owen is a manager for a financial services company. Several months ago, he realized he wanted to improve his skills in interviewing job candidates. He defined an achievable goal. He made it his goal to prepare a list of questions in advance for the next five job positions for which he interviewed candidates. He also chose a mentor within his company to critique his questions.

See each aspect of Owen's goal to learn about the benefits he gained by setting it.

Guiding decisions

"My goal guided my decisions and actions. When I browsed newspapers or magazines, I chose to read articles I found about interviewing. I prepared a list of questions in advance for interviews, and I asked Susan, a human resources specialist, to critique them."

Monitoring progress

"I measured my progress by the number of questions my mentor rejected. In the first list I compiled, she threw out six questions. When I showed her questions I'd prepared for the next open position, she only rejected two. I could see my questions were getting better."

Communicating growth

"I discussed my goal and my progress in reaching it with my supervisor. My interest in improving my skills showed him I'm interested in the quality of job candidates we hire. Our discussions also allowed me to ask for more opportunities to use my improved skills."

Question

The first step in most significant accomplishments is defining an achievable goal.

Identify the benefits of defining achievable goals.

Options:

1. They provide a tool to guide work-related decisions.
2. They allow you to monitor your own progress.
3. They provide a basis for communicating with others about how you perform your job.
4. They provide a way for supervisors to review your job performance.
5. They help you achieve objectives you thought were unattainable.

Answer:

Achievable goals guide your decisions and help you determine how you're progressing toward your destination. Your goals also give you a framework for communicating about your accomplishments and plans.

Option 1: This is a correct option. An achievable goal guides your daily work-related decisions and the actions that follow. When you have a clear goal, you can make decisions and take actions that will help you achieve it.

Option 2: This is a correct choice. An achievable goal provides a standard measurement for monitoring your own progress toward a desired accomplishment. As you draw nearer to reaching your goal, you can realize how much progress you've already made.

Option 3: This is a correct option. An achievable goal gives you a framework for communicating with supervisors and coworkers about your accomplishments and your plans for the future.

Option 4: This is not a correct option. Goals are not the same thing as accomplishments. Your job performance is measured by your accomplishments. Your goals describe what you intend to accomplish.

Option 5: This is not a correct choice. For a goal to be achievable, it must also be believable. An achievable goal describes accomplishments you believe are within your grasp.

An achievable goal is more than a destination. It's also a tool that helps you take the shortest path to your destination.

In this lesson, you'll explore two distinct, but interrelated types of goals you can set for yourself, and you'll examine what goes into an achievable goal.

PERFORMANCE GOALS AND DEVELOPMENT GOALS

Performance goals and development goals

In some science fiction novels and movies, the future of work is bleak. Work in the future is often portrayed as dull, repetitive, and dehumanizing.

Opportunities for change, challenge, and growth make work and life more interesting and fulfilling. When writers and moviemakers want to depict a dreary future, they describe a future without these opportunities.

Your work-related goals provide opportunities for change, challenge, and growth. There are two different types of personal goals you can set to enhance your career and personal life:

- performance,
- development.

Performance goals set standards for results you want to achieve in your regular activities. These goals usually set targets that challenge your existing abilities and require you to stretch them to new levels of achievement.

Performance goals describe a change from your current level of performance to the targeted level and the time period in which the change will happen.

You're probably familiar with performance goals. You may have set many performance goals for yourself in your professional and personal life.

See the examples of performance goals for more information about them.

Example 1

A sales representative for a commercial printing firm sets a goal to increase sales to her current clients by $400,000 for the calendar year. She'll have to exercise her creative ability and her persuasiveness to achieve this goal.

Example 2

The assembly line manager for an automaker sets performance goals to reduce the dollar value of parts in inventory by 3 percent within 90 days. He will have to stretch his planning ability to attain the goal.

Example 3

A swimmer sets a performance goal to reduce her average time to swim 100 meters by a half second before a swim meet. She'll have to improve her strength and swimming technique to reduce her time.

Development goals describe plans to acquire new abilities or to enhance existing abilities. These new or enhanced abilities are acquired through some type of learning activity: gaining on-the-job experience, working with a mentor, or taking an academic course or training class.

A development goal often includes a time frame for the learning activity or a deadline to give the goal urgency.

The purpose of a development goal is to expand your capabilities. In your professional life, development goals help you prepare to take on new job responsibilities. In your personal life, development goals allow you to make life more rewarding and interesting.

See the examples for further explanation about development goals.

Example 1

An assistant buyer for a department store sets a goal to develop her skill in managing merchandise. She will gain on-the-job experience by placing orders for merchandise. She will be ready to manage her own department at the end of the year.

Example 2

An environmental engineer sets a development goal to improve his ability to lead meetings. He will receive mentoring from an experienced colleague. The colleague will review the engineer's plans for conducting five meetings and will critique the plans.

Example 3

An information systems manager sets a development goal to learn how to manage her personal finances. She will take a night class in financial management at the local community college. She will begin applying her new knowledge immediately.

Performance goals and development goals are often interrelated. A performance goal may require an associated development goal because new or enhanced skills will be needed to attain the targeted performance level.

Recall the commercial printing sales representative who set a performance goal to increase sales. She may set an accompanying development goal to take a time-management course as a tool to help her reach her sales goal.

A performance goal can also be used to help you determine whether you've successfully achieved a development goal. The department store assistant buyer set a performance goal to prepare monthly purchasing plans for eight categories of merchandise for the next three months.

She will complete the plans in the same amount of time allowed for senior buyers. If she can attain this performance goal, she will have evidence that she also attained her development goal.

Question

The two different types of personal goals you can set are performance goals and development goals.

Which are examples of development goals?

Options:

1. Increase sales to current clients by 11 percent for the fiscal year.

2. Train two subordinates to prepare accurate profit projections within six months.

3. Complete a self-study course in active listening skills by the end of the year.

4. Seek coaching from a project manager on scheduling skills.

5. Perform on-site visits with eight clients to gain experience resolving client problems.

Answer:

Performance goals set standards for acceptable performance of a job. Development goals describe training, job experience, or coaching that help you acquire new skills or improve your existing skills.

Option 1: This is an example of a performance goal. It sets a target for a measurable change in the results produced by a salesperson within a specific time frame. A development of new abilities or skills is not specified.

Option 2: This is a performance goal. This goal sets measurable results for performing a specific task within a given time frame. It does not specify new abilities or skills to be acquired by the person who must perform the task.

Option 3: This is a development goal. It describes an educational activity that creates new abilities or enhances existing abilities for the person who completes the task. The deadline gives the development goal urgency.

Option 4: This is a development goal. The purpose of this goal is to improve a specific skill or ability. Coaching from an expert is one of several ways to gain new abilities or expand existing abilities.

Option 5: This is a development goal. This goal describes direct job experience for the purpose of acquiring a specific skill. The required number of on-site visits provides a measurable way to ensure the goal has been addressed.

Goals are a way of managing change. Without change and the challenges it brings, life would be monotonous.

Performance goals raise your aim and take full advantage your current abilities. Development goals expand your abilities and prepare you for new opportunities.

ACHIEVABLE AND UNACHIEVABLE GOALS

Achievable and unachievable goals

Why do people so often fail to keep their New Year's resolutions? Many times it's because they've set goals for themselves that can't be achieved.

Achievable goals have two required components: an objective component and a standards component. A third optional component--a conditions component--may also be included to support the required components.

The objective component describes a specific activity that will be performed by the person trying to achieve the goal.

A goal must have an objective component to be achievable.

Here are several examples of activities described in objective components of goals: • Increase sales for a service.
  • Reduce costs of materials.
  • Complete a course in a specific subject.

- Submit a plan for implementing a procedure. • Write a report that describes a process.
- Teach staff to perform a task.
- Conduct interviews to gather information.

A standards component measures whether an objective has been reached. Common types of standards include a count of successful results, a degree of change, or a deadline for completion. A goal may include more than one standards component. Here are some examples of standards components:

- within six weeks
- eight times successfully
- by 30 percent
- less than five occurrences
- varying by less than 5 percent

The conditions component is any phrase that sharpens the focus of goals. Conditions components are used as needed to clarify the objective or limit the way in which it can be achieved.

Two examples of goals consisting of an objective component and a standards component are given. Select each goal to add a conditions component that modifies the goal.

Goal 1

Condition: Without increasing the number of product defects. This condition puts a limit on the effects of reducing materials cost.

Goal 2

Condition: Select staff members with the most seniority. This condition narrows the choice of which staff members can be trained to fulfill the objective.

Question

Doing Business Professionally

Chuck is a business analyst for an environmental engineering firm. He must set an achievable goal that will help him develop his business analysis skills. Match the components of an achievable goal with one or more examples.

Options:
A. objective component
B. standards component
C. conditions component

Targets:
1. complete a college-level course in business statistics
2. earning a grade of B or higher
3. without taking time off from work
4. during the next academic term

Answer:
The correct answers are indicated. Taking a course is an action or objective. Earning a grade of B or higher and completing the course in the next term are standards components. Not taking time off from work is a relevant condition.

This is the objective component of Chuck's goal because it describes the activity he will perform and complete. An objective component is a required element of an achievable goal.

This is a standards component of Chuck's goal. The minimum acceptable grade defines what constitutes successful achievement of the goal.

This is a conditions component. It describes a relevant condition for the completion of Chuck's goal. Relevant conditions aren't required, but they may be used to set limits on the measures that may be applied to achieve a goal.

This is a standards component that describes how quickly the goal must be completed. A goal may have more than one standards component.

Each of these components must be used appropriately to create an achievable goal. For instance, the objective component of an achievable goal should describe an outcome that is within the control of the goal seeker.

If achieving the goal depends on the actions or decisions of others, attaining the goal isn't entirely within your control.

The activity or result described in an objective component should be something you can observe and measure.

If you can't observe and measure the result, it will be difficult to know whether you've attained the goal.

Brian is a sales representative for a grain milling company. He worked on setting personal goals for the coming year. He's considered the listed objective components. Which of the objective components do you think are appropriate for Brian to use?

See each of the objective components to discover if you answered correctly.

Increase sales in the assigned territory

This is an appropriate objective component. Brian controls his own results by calling on customers and making convincing sales presentations. The results of those efforts can be measured by the dollar value of the products sold.

Achieve the highest team sales

This is not an appropriate objective component. Brian can't control how hard other sales representatives work or what level of sales they achieve. Their actions affect whether Brian achieves the highest team sales.

Write a report that describes a billing process

This is an appropriate objective component. Brian controls how much time he spends gathering data and writing the report. He doesn't depend on anyone else to achieve the objective. The result can be observed and measured in terms of how quickly he produces the report.

Understand how the billing process works

This is not an appropriate objective component. Brian's understanding of the billing process isn't something that can be observed or measured. If Brian creates an objective that demonstrates his understanding, such as writing a report, that would be an appropriate objective.

When you create a standards component for a goal, it should describe how you will measure the activity or results in your objective component. You also set a specific target--a percentage, count, or time--that you're striving to achieve.

Your standards component must also reflect realistic expectations. Your target level of achievement should challenge you to do your best, but it should also leave a little room for inevitable mistakes. Nobody's perfect.

Brian, the milling company sales representative, proposed standards components in each of his personal goals. His standards components are listed along with their related objectives. Examine each one and determine whether it's appropriate within an achievable goal.

See each of the standards components to check your answer.

Increase sales in the assigned territory by 8% over last year

This is an appropriate standards component. The objective, increasing sales, will be measured by calculating the percentage sales increase over the previous year. The target level of achievement is very specific--8 percent.

Increase sales in an assigned territory by a significant percentage over last year

This is not an appropriate standards component. The method of measuring sales increases is adequately described--the increase will be calculated as a percentage change from the previous year. However, the target of a "significant percentage" is not specific.

Write a report that describes the billing process and contains no errors

This is not an appropriate standards component. Even an expert on the company's billing system may be unable to prepare a report that's entirely free of errors. This standards component sets a target for success that isn't realistic.

Within four weeks, complete a report describing the billing process, and submit it to the supervisor

This is an appropriate standards component if Brian can realistically expect to complete his report in four weeks. This standards component measures the report writing activity in terms of how long it takes to complete. The standard for success is specific at four weeks.

Conditions components are limitations on how you achieve your objective. Use them when there are activities or results that must be included or avoided as you pursue your goal.

If some possible activities for achieving your goal will cause harm or create new problems, a conditions component limits your choices. The potentially harmful activities are specifically excluded.

Brian needs to add a conditions component to his goal to increase sales within his territory by 8 percent over last year. Two possible conditions components for this goal are given. Which of the conditions components do you think is appropriate to make his goal more achievable?

See each of the conditions components to check your answer.

while maintaining current profit margins

This is an appropriate conditions component because it limits how Brian can achieve his sales goal. He can't make sales at a lower profit margin to increase his sales.

while adding new accounts

This isn't an appropriate conditions component because it doesn't narrow or clarify the objective of increasing sales. It's just an additional objective.

Question

Evelyn is a shipping supervisor for a software company. She wants to be promoted to assistant operations manager this year. She resolved to quell conflicts among her subordinates and encourage them to be more productive. Evelyn has set several personal goals. Which goals are unachievable?

Options:

1. Reduce late deliveries to customers to 10 percent this year without increasing costs.

2. Develop more willingness to accept constructive criticism in the months ahead.

3. Win a promotion to the next open slot for an assistant operations manager.

4. Reduce the number of employee conflicts to zero during the next fiscal year.

5. Create measurable growth in employee commitment to this quarter's sales goal.

Answer:

The correct answers are indicated. Evelyn's achievable goal includes an objective that defines actions and results within her control. It includes a standard for measuring whether the goal was achieved. Conditions may be applied if they're relevant.

Option 1: This is an achievable goal. Reducing the number of late deliveries is an objective that defines Evelyn's actions. The standard for achieving the goal is set at less than 10 percent. Keeping costs down is a relevant condition.

Option 2: This is not an achievable goal. Accepting constructive criticism is a passive, not active behavior. It's also impossible to directly observe or measure Evelyn's willingness to accept criticism.

Option 3: This is not an achievable goal. Although Evelyn can control her own actions to qualify for a promotion, she can't control who is selected. An achievable goal should depend only on actions Evelyn controls.

Option 4: This goal is not achievable. Evelyn can't control whether conflicts between other people occur. An achievable goal contains an objective component that defines the actions of the person who must attempt the goal.

Option 5: This is not an achievable goal. Simply including the word "measurable" in the goal doesn't make the goal realistic or meaningful. Evelyn can't directly observe or measure her subordinates' commitment to the company's goals.

If you set your goals properly and include the necessary components, you'll have a better chance of success. Appropriate objective and standards components are required, and conditions components are often helpful.

USING STRATEGIC THINKING TO SET GOALS

Using strategic thinking to set goals

There's more to setting a goal than simply choosing a destination you want to reach. Setting goals requires strategic thinking to help you anticipate obstacles and collaboration with people who can help you overcome those obstacles.

When you practice strategic thinking as you set goals, you gain several important benefits.

A majority of your work-related goals require participation from others in your organization. Strategic thinking helps you identify people who can help you achieve your goals so you can gain their cooperation.

Strategic thinking also helps you assess the risks in your goals more accurately. Taking on too much risk can cause you to fail to reach your goals. Taking on too little risk may mean you're not challenging yourself.

By thinking strategically about your goals, you gain a clear picture of how much risk you're assuming.

Finally, strategic thinking helps you set goals in ways that reduce wasted effort. When you apply strategic thinking in setting your goals, you're better prepared to recognize risks and potential conflicts and take steps to avoid them or cope with them.

As a result, you're less likely to spend your time on unproductive activities. When you think strategically in setting your goals, you're better able to focus on activities that help you reach your goals.

Sharon is an information systems manager for a chain of discount shoe stores. Last year she set a goal to teach store managers how to use the company's computerized inventory tracking system to send reorder requests to the central purchasing office. Sharon applied strategic thinking to improve the achievability of her goal.

See each aspect of strategic thinking for Sharon's description of the benefits of strategic thinking when setting goals.

Collaboration

"Our company operates more than 300 stores in 25 states. I couldn't train all of the store managers by myself. To achieve my goal, I needed to collaborate with the director of stores. Without his help, reaching my goal would have been impossible."

Risk

"I realized there was a risk that giving store managers new capabilities might conflict with the central purchasing office's goal to narrow the assortment of shoe styles in our stores. I made sure my training wouldn't conflict with that goal"

Productivity

"Thinking strategically about my goal helped me use my time productively. I developed my training session with help from the director of stores and I presented it to the central purchasing staff. These steps helped me avoid mistakes that could derail my progress."

Question

Thinking strategically as you set goals provides several important benefits.

Identify the benefits of using strategic thinking to set goals.

Options:

1. It's easier to win cooperation from others in achieving your goals.

2. You more accurately assess the risks related to your goals.

3. It reduces the amount of wasted or unproductive effort you spend in pursuing your goals.

4. You reduce the risk of encountering obstacles that may prevent you from achieving your goals.

5. You gain a competitive advantage over others who seek conflicting goals.

Answer:

Strategic thinking in goal setting helps you clearly understand potential obstacles and risks you face. It can also help you identify potential partners who will collaborate with you. As a result, less of your effort will be wasted or unproductive.

Option 1: This is a correct option. Applying strategic thinking in your goal setting helps you align your goals with the goals of others. When your goals align with the goals of others, they're more likely to help you reach your goals.

Option 2: This is a correct choice. Applying strategic thinking gives you a more accurate assessment of the amount of risk in the goals you've set. The potential rewards of achieving a goal are directly related to the amount of risk involved.

Option 3: This is a correct choice. Strategic thinking in goal setting helps you identify potential risks and obstacles that can cause wasted or unproductive effort. Strategic thinking also helps you identify potential allies who can make achieving your goals easier.

Option 4: This is not a correct option. Strategic thinking won't make potential obstacles go away. It will help you recognize obstacles and plan how you'll deal with them.

Option 5: This is not a correct option. The purpose of strategic thinking in goal setting is to align your own goals with the goals of others. Collaboration, not competition, is the benefit of strategic thinking.

Thinking strategically is an essential part of setting achievable goals. Without strategic thinking, you're not likely to find the most direct path to your destination.

ASSESSING THE AMOUNT OF RISK

Assessing the amount of risk

The purpose of setting a goal is to gain a reward. However, striving for a goal means you must also accept the risk of failure.

Setting any work-related goal requires an investment of time and effort. If you attain your goal, your investment results in success. However, there's always a risk you'll fail to achieve a goal and your time and effort will be lost.

The amount of risk in a goal correlates to the time and effort required to achieve it. Low-risk goals usually require a small amount of investment of time and effort. High-risk goals often require a large investment of time and effort.

Both high-risk and low-risk goals are appropriate types of work-related goals. However, you probably pursue more than one goal at a time. Assessing the combined risk of all your goals can help you evaluate whether you're investing your time and effort wisely.

See each level of risk to learn more about it.

High risk

If many of your goals are high-risk goals, their combined potential rewards may be very large. However, too many high-risk goals may overtax your resources.

Low risk

If many of your goals are low risk, there's less opportunity for failure, but low-risk goals aren't as challenging and don't offer big rewards.

To assess the combined risk of all of the goals you're pursuing at any time, first classify each individual goal as high risk or low risk.

To classify each goal, you must examine how achieving your goal requires you to change conditions that exist to conditions you want. As the time and effort to create a change increases, so does the risk associated with your goal.

There are four different ways goals describe a change in existing conditions to desired conditions. Two types of change are associated with high-risk goals.

See each type of change associated with high-risk goals to learn more about it.

Create

Creating a new condition requires you to acquire an entirely new skill or accomplish something that hasn't been done before. The desired conditions don't yet exist, so a goal seeker is responsible for a high degree of change.

Eliminate

Eliminating an existing condition is like putting out a fire. A condition exists that needs to be ended. Elimination objectives carry a high degree of risk because they may cause unforeseen results and can disrupt the work of others.

Ron is a news producer for a television station. He has created a set of goals that he wants to accomplish in the upcoming year.

Before he can assess how much risk all of his goals represent together, he must classify each goal as high risk or low risk.

Ron set a goal to create a new weekly feature segment for his station's news program. The new feature will profile local artists and musicians. The station doesn't run any similar features, so Ron will have to plan the series, win approval, write the segments, and supervise taping.

Ron classified this as a high-risk goal because he will have to create the new series of feature segments from the beginning. He has to create a condition--airing a series of feature segments--that doesn't currently exist.

Ron also set a goal to end the need for daily noon meetings with his news production team. Ron has decided that the meetings aren't productive.

He considers this a high-risk goal because he's eliminating an existing condition--the meetings that have been held every day for many years will cease. Ron will have to make sure eliminating the meetings doesn't deprive his team members of information they need to do their jobs.

The remaining two types of change are associated with low-risk goals.

See each type of change associated with low-risk goals to learn more about it.

Preserve

Preserving an existing condition requires you to make marginal changes or improvements to results that have already been achieved. Preserving an existing condition is a low-risk goal because you're working to keep results that already exist.

Avoid

Avoiding an unwanted condition requires you to keep errors or other negative events from taking place. This reflects a low-risk goal because the condition you want already exists. Your goal is to avoid exceptions or changes.

Ron holds his production team to a rigid deadline. All recorded news stories are complete and ready to broadcast 20 minutes before the broadcast begins. The team was successful in meeting this deadline 96 percent of the time last year. Ron set a goal to increase that to 98 percent of the time.

This goal preserves an existing condition, so Ron considers it a low-risk goal. The condition for success--meeting the deadline--already exists. Ron only has to take steps to marginally improve that condition to achieve his goal.

One of Ron's duties as a news producer is to make sure to prepare enough news stories for a 30-minute program. Ron set a goal to provide the right amount of news content to avoid having any night's program run more than ten seconds too long or too short.

This is a low-risk goal for Ron. He has to use existing methods to avoid an unwanted condition.

Question

Different goals carry different degrees of risk. The objective components of five goals are shown below. Match the type of risk to one or more goals.

Options:
A. high risk
B. low risk

Targets:
1. Complete a course to learn to speak a foreign language.
2. Reduce the number of positions in the data entry department from eight to four.
3. Complete a self-study course to enhance writing skill.
4. Maintain employee turnover at the current rate of less than 5 percent.
5. Prevent payroll costs from rising above current levels.

Answer:
High-risk goals create something entirely new or eliminate a condition that currently exists. Low-risk goals seek to keep things the way they are or make incremental changes.

This is an example of a high-risk goal. Learning to speak a foreign language involves acquiring an entirely new skill. You'll have to invest a lot of effort to realize your goal.

This goal is a high-risk goal. This goal requires eliminating four data entry positions that currently exist. There's a high degree of risk that eliminating the jobs could have unforeseen consequences.

This is an example of a low-risk goal. This goal doesn't require the acquisition of entirely new skills. It modifies a skill that already exists. There is very little risk that the goal seeker's writing will become worse as a result.

This is a low-risk goal. This goal preserves a condition that already exists. Unless new challenges emerge, achieving this goal will not require major changes in activities or strategies.

This goal carries a low amount of risk. The desired level of success has already been achieved. This goal seeks only to avoid a change in current conditions. New activities or strategies aren't likely to be needed.

To assess the combined risk in a set of goals, count the number of high-risk and low-risk goals. The combined risk is balanced between high-risk and low-risk goals if there is the same number of each type of goal.

If the number of high-risk goals exceeds the number of low-risk goals, you're aggressive in assuming risk. A difference of one goal is somewhat aggressive. A difference of two or more goals is very aggressive.

If you set more low-risk goals than high-risk goals, you're being cautious in taking on risk. A difference of just one goal indicates you're somewhat cautious. A difference of two or more is a sign you're being very cautious.

Beware of hidden or unstated goals. For example, if you're constantly struggling to cover all of your job duties or meet schedules, you probably have an unstated goal to improve your performance in those areas.

If you discover that you have unstated goals, include them in your count of high-risk goals. That will force you to be more cautious in assuming risks in your stated goals to bring their combined risk into balance.

Ron, the news producer, classified each of his goals as high risk or low risk.

He counted his goals to create a new feature segment and to eliminate mid-day meetings as high-risk goals. He counted his goals to maintain deadlines and avoid variances in the length of newscasts as low-risk goals.

As long as Ron doesn't have any unstated goals, the combined risk in his goals is balanced between high-risk and low-risk goals. However, if he recognizes that he has an unstated goal and counts it as a high-risk goal, his overall risk is somewhat aggressive.

Case Study: Question 1 of 2

Scenario

Isabel is a real estate manager for a restaurant company. She recently made a list of work-related goals she wants to accomplish within the next year.

Isabel finds her job challenging, but she is able to fulfill her job duties and complete projects on time. She wants to earn an advanced degree in finance, but she hasn't yet decided when she will take the required classes.

Answer the questions in order.

Question:

Isabel's proposed work-related goals are listed below. Match the type of risk to one or more of Isabel's goals.

Options:

A. low risk
B. high risk

Targets:

1. Keep rent costs at the current level of 6 percent of gross sales.
2. Increase the number of contracts for new sites from 15 last year to 18 this year.
3. Visit five construction sites to upgrade skills in estimating construction schedules.
4. Decrease the time between site selection and the start of construction by 5 percent.
5. Create a way to estimate the impact of nearby competitors on restaurant sales.

Answer:

The correct answers are indicated. Most of Isabel's goals are low risk and describe incremental changes over previous results. Only the development of a way to estimate the impact of competing restaurants is a high-risk goal.

This is a low-risk goal. The desired level of rent cost has already been achieved. As long as there are no dramatic changes expected in rent costs, setting a goal to maintain that level involves a low amount of risk.

This goal has a low degree of risk. This goal requires Isabel to make an incremental change over her previous performance. That means this is a low-risk goal.

This is a low-risk goal. Isabel set this goal to further develop a skill she already practices. This incremental change to an existing skill carries a low risk of failure for the amount of effort it requires.

This goal carries low risk. This goal is an incremental change compared to current performance. Isabel's starting point is already very close to her goal.

This is a high-risk goal. This goal requires Isabel to develop a sales evaluation method that's needed but doesn't yet exist. It's likely that Isabel will have to invest a significant effort to achieve her goal.

Case Study: Question 2 of 2

What is the level of risk in Isabel's set of proposed goals?

Options:
1. very cautious
2. somewhat cautious
3. balanced
4. somewhat aggressive
5. very aggressive

Answer:

Isabel's proposed goals include four low-risk goals and only one high-risk goal. Her job circumstances don't require any restriction on risk. Her proposed goals carry a very cautious level of risk.

Option 1: This is the correct option. Isabel proposed four low-risk goals and only one high-risk goal.

The circumstances of her job don't require her to minimize her risks. She has been very cautious in assuming risk.

Option 2: This is not the correct choice. If Isabel's goals were tilted only slightly in favor of low-risk goals, her level of risk would be somewhat cautious. However, her goals were heavily skewed toward low-risk goals.

Option 3: This is not the correct option. Isabel's level of risk would be balanced if she chose the same number of high-risk and low-risk goals. However, her proposed goals are tilted heavily in one direction.

Option 4: This is not the correct choice. Isabel's goals would carry a somewhat aggressive level of risk if she had chosen slightly more high-risk goals than low-risk goals. However, she chose far more low-risk goals.

Option 5: This isn't the correct choice. Isabel's goals would include a very aggressive level of risk if she had set many more high-risk goals than low-risk goals. Her proposed goals tilt the other way.

Isabel has set far more low-risk goals than high-risk goals. She's being very cautious about taking risks.

Once Isabel assesses the combined risk in all of her goals, she can decide whether she's being too cautious. Too much caution may keep her from setting challenging and potentially rewarding goals.

Assessing risk is an important part of setting goals. However, there's no level of risk that's right for everyone.

It's up to you to decide how much risk you're willing to accept to achieve your goals.

A COLLABORATIVE GOAL

A collaborative goal

Some goals may seem too hard to achieve on your own.

When you need help to achieve a goal, that's a good time to find a partner with whom you can collaborate.

The people who can help you achieve your goals won't always share your goals. Their goals may even conflict with yours. You can resolve conflicts and build partnerships by applying these steps to create a collaborative goal:
- Define the conflict.
- Propose a collaboration.
- Define collaborative roles.

The first step in creating a collaborative goal is defining conflicts between your goals and the goals of another member of your organization.

Describe your own goal in terms of what you need to accomplish. Then ask the other person to describe the need she seeks to fulfill by achieving her conflicting goal.

Defining conflicting goals is an information-gathering step. Use this step to learn as much as you can about the other person's goal.

Define the conflict by learning what the other person needs to accomplish. This helps you avoid making the conflict personal. A conflicting goal isn't a personal attack. It's an opportunity for innovation and collaboration.

If you focus on what you need and what Dwight needs, the conflict between your goals and his is less likely to become a personal conflict. Discussing needs gives Dwight an opportunity to help you.

The next step in creating a collaborative goal is to propose the collaboration. Propose a single goal that addresses your own needs as well as the needs of the other party. Make your suggestion and ask for the other person's opinion.

Resist the urge to seek an advantage over the person who holds the conflicting goal. Don't try to argue that your goal is more important or more urgent. Respect your coworker's right to pursue goals of her own.

Proposing a collaboration isn't the same as suggesting a compromise. When two people with conflicting goals compromise, neither gets what he wants.

A collaborative goal creates a way for both parties to achieve their goals.

The final step in creating a collaborative goal is to define roles for the participants in the collaboration. The roles for the participants should be equal. Neither participant should assume authority over the other. Both participants should contribute equal amounts of effort and receive equal benefit.

Collaboration means working together. The roles for the participants in a collaborative goal should begin at the same time and involve as many shared activities as possible. When you propose roles, clearly define what both parties will contribute. If you don't, you haven't created a real collaboration.

Avoid proposing a collaboration that requires one participant to complete her share of the work before the other participant begins. That may create a perception that one participant is allowed to delay his work until later.

Case Study: Question 1 of 3
Scenario:

Simon is a project manager for a software company. His goal is to reduce the development time for a new software product by 15 days.

However, Erica, the director of product testing, wants to schedule more testing time instead of less.

Simon must forge a collaborative goal with Erica if he wants to achieve his own goal. Answer the questions in order.

Question:

What should Simon say to initiate a discussion with Erica to seek a collaborative goal?

Options:

1. I need to shorten the deadline for delivering our new product. I understand you want to increase testing time. Why do you need to do that?

2. I understand you want to increase the amount of testing time for new products. That's going to cause serious problems for me. What can I do to change your decision?

3. Your plan is to increase testing time. Isn't that likely to increase costs as well?

4. You want to increase testing time and I want to finish the project more quickly. Our goals seem to be incompatible, don't they?

Answer:

Simon should explain the need behind his goal, and then invite Erica to do the same. This provides a basis for finding a shared objective.

Option 1: This is the correct choice. This message summarizes what Simon needs to accomplish, and then asks Erica to describe the need that will be fulfilled by her conflicting goal. This is the information Simon needs to find a collaborative goal.

Option 2: This is not the correct choice. If Simon begins this way, he's attempting to negotiate a solution before he learns what motivates Erica. This isn't the best way for Simon to begin searching for a collaborative goal.

Option 3: This isn't the correct option. This choice contains a leading question that may limit the conversation that follows. Simon should prompt Erica to explain the need her goal fulfills.

Option 4: This is not the correct choice. Simon's question suggests only one goal can succeed. Creating a situation in which one party wins and the other loses is not a basis for collaboration.

Case Study: Question 2 of 3

Erica explains that customer complaints about errors in new software releases have increased. She needs to prevent those errors from going undetected. That's why she wants to increase testing for new products.

What should Simon say to continue?

Options:

1. Suppose we set a goal to increase the amount of testing, but with an earlier deadline. Would that help you fulfill your need to reduce defects?

2. If I relax my goal and reduce testing time by only 5 percent, would you be willing to modify your goal to the same degree?

3. Reducing the cost of testing is in the company's best interest. How will your goal contribute to a reduction in testing cost?

4. Maybe your problem isn't the amount of time you have for testing. Is there a way for you to improve your department's efficiency?

Answer:

Simon should propose a goal that meets Erica's needs as well as his own. At this point in the conversation, Simon can take the lead by making suggestions that will elicit ideas from Erica.

Option 1: This is the correct choice. Simon proposes a single objective with an agreed standard. The shared goal isn't a compromise, but a goal that fulfills both parties' needs.

Option 2: This is not a correct option. Simon shouldn't compromise on the standards he set for his goal. Instead, he should suggest a goal that will meet Erica's needs as well as his own.

Option 3: This is not the correct choice. Lower costs may be in the company's best interest, but so is a reduction in defects. Simon should not attempt to focus the conversation only on his own objective.

Option 4: This is not the correct choice. Questioning Erica's competence in setting her own goals won't promote collaboration. In fact, it will probably decrease her willingness to cooperate.

Case Study: Question 3 of 3

Erica agrees that performing more hours of testing but imposing an earlier deadline is feasible and would meet her needs.

What should Simon say to continue seeking collaboration?

Options:

1. I'll see if there are software testers we can borrow from other projects. Will you develop a schedule that shows how much additional help you'll need?

2. Why don't you see if you can create a testing schedule that allows your staff to spend the hours needed in fewer days?

3. I'll ask some of the other project managers if they can spare any of their software testers to help you get the work done more quickly. Would that help you?

4. I'll draw up a new project schedule that meets both our needs and I'll send you a copy. After you review it, let me know what you need to meet the new schedule.

Answer:

The correct answer is indicated. Simon should propose roles for himself and Erica that require them both to start working toward the same goal as soon as possible.

Option 1: This is the correct option. This proposal requires both Simon and Erica to work toward their collaborative goal. For a collaborative goal to work, both parties must contribute equally.

Option 2: This is not the correct choice. Simon should propose roles for himself and for Erica. Otherwise, it might appear he's asking Erica to do all the work to achieve the collaborative goal.

Option 3: This is not the correct choice. For a collaborative goal to work, both parties must contribute. Simon should propose a role for Erica as well as one for himself.

Option 4: This is not the correct choice. Simon should suggest a role for Erica that gets her involved right away. This proposal delays her involvement until later.

To gain Erica's cooperation in helping him complete the software project more quickly, Simon needed to apply the three steps for creating a collaborative goal.

He had to first define how their goals differed, next establish a shared goal that met both of their needs, and lastly propose roles that would help them achieve that goal.

With strategic collaboration, the person who seems to be an obstacle in your path can become an ally, a partner in attaining your goal.

ALIGNING PERSONAL PRIORITIES WITH GOALS

Aligning personal priorities with goals

There's a big difference between a goal and an accomplishment. Setting a goal is the beginning of a process. If you're successful, an accomplishment comes at the end of the process.

Question

The process that takes you from a goal to an accomplishment involves hard work and perseverance. Your chances of achieving a goal depend on how well you assess the work that needs to be done and your ability to align your priorities with your goals.

What percentage of the goals you set do you successfully achieve?

Options:

1. 0 percent
2. 25 percent
3. 50 percent
4. 75 percent
5. 100 percent

Answer:

Option 1: One of the most common reasons people fail to achieve goals is that they try to accomplish more than they're able to. To set a goal that's achievable, you have to allocate your limited resources effectively.

Option 2: One of the most common reasons people fail to achieve goals is that they try to accomplish more than they're able to. To set a goal that's achievable, you have to allocate your limited resources effectively.

Option 3: One of the most common reasons people fail to achieve goals is that they try to accomplish more than they're able to. To set a goal that's achievable, you have to allocate your limited resources effectively.

Option 4: One of the most common reasons people fail to achieve goals is that they try to accomplish more than they're able to. To set a goal that's achievable, you have to allocate your limited resources effectively.

Option 5: One of the most common reasons people fail to achieve goals is that they try to accomplish more than they're able to. To set a goal that's achievable, you have to allocate your limited resources effectively.

There are several benefits that come from aligning your priorities and your goals. When your priorities accurately reflect your goals, you're more likely to get started and do what's needed to achieve important or urgent goals. You're less likely to procrastinate or to delay in taking action.

Prioritizing actions that will help you achieve your goals leads to another benefit: you achieve goals more quickly. When your priorities align with your goals, you don't have to wait as long to realize the rewards of your work.

Keeping your priorities and goals aligned also helps you recognize when it's time to let go of a goal. If your goal no longer seems to be worth a top-priority effort, it's time to reassess your priorities or set an alternative goal.

Roberta is a marketing manager for a consumer products company. She set a goal to develop her listening skills and she succeeded. She believes that aligning her priorities with that goal made the difference.

See each of Roberta's explanations to learn more about her experience.

Explanation 1

"When I set a goal to improve my listening skills, I made that goal one of my top priorities. When I found a self-study course on the subject, I took it right away."

Explanation 2

"Improving my listening skills has been something I've been meaning to do for years. Once I aligned my priorities with that goal, I achieved it in just a couple of months."

Roberta had originally wanted to develop her listening skills by attending a three-day seminar led by a popular author and psychologist. However, she could never find the time in her schedule--or the money to pay the expensive tuition fee--when the seminar was being offered.

When she aligned her priorities with her goal, she realized it was time to let go of her original plan and find an alternative.

Question

Aligning your priorities with your goals is beneficial in several ways.

Identify the benefits of aligning your priorities with your goals.

Options:
1. You achieve your goals more quickly.
2. You take action on important or urgent goals first.
3. You're better able to recognize when it's time to let go of a goal, or choose an alternative to goals that prove unattainable.
4. You're able to devote all of your energy to attaining your goals.
5. You have fewer reasons to reconsider or change your goals.

Answer:

Actually, aligning your priorities with goals helps focus your attention and clarify the reasons for setting a goal. You'll reach goals more quickly, prioritize action on important or urgent goals, and recognize suitable alternatives to your goals.

Option 1: This is a correct choice. When you align your priorities with your goals, you address more of your efforts to achieving your goals. As a result, you attain your goals more quickly.

Option 2: This is a correct option. When you align your priorities with your goals, you place a higher priority on activities that help you achieve your goals. Naturally, goals that are more important or urgent will receive a higher priority.

Option 3: This is a correct choice. Aligning your priorities with your goals will help you recognize why your goals are important to you. When you understand what makes a goal important, you're better able to find an alternative to meet the same needs.

Option 4: This is not a correct option. Aligning your priorities and goals will help you focus your attention on your goals. However, this process won't make all your mundane chores and obligations go away.

Option 5: This is an incorrect option. Aligning your priorities and goals will help you allocate your time to achieving your goals. However, this process won't keep obstacles from arising that require you to reconsider or change goals.

Aligning your priorities and goals is a valuable tool in your goal-setting process.

In this lesson, you'll examine how to compare your goals against each other and prioritize each one.

You'll also explore strategies for choosing alternative goals when your progress is blocked. You'll learn how to preserve what was important in your original goal while choosing a new path to achieve it.

PRIORITIZING GOALS

Prioritizing goals

Few people enjoy the luxury of pursuing only one goal at a time. Most have to juggle several goals simultaneously.

When you pursue several goals at once, you have to prioritize some goals ahead of others. There are two elements that determine the priority you assign to any goal:
- the importance or value of achieving the goal,
- the availability of resources needed to reach the goal.

The potential rewards you and your organization receive for achieving a goal determine the importance or value of the goal. There are two factors to consider when you evaluate the importance of a goal-- personal importance and professional importance.

See each factor to consider to learn more about it.

Personal importance

A goal has a high level of personal importance when achieving the goal satisfies your own values or desires. It means that achieving the goal matters to you.

Professional importance

A goal has professional importance when achieving it satisfies the duties or requirements of your job. It means achieving the goal matters to your employer.

Warren is an account representative for a company that sells employee identification systems. He set several goals for the coming year. His goals don't have the same level of importance.

See each of Warren's goals listed below for his explanation of how they differ in their importance.

Update customer contact information in the company sales database.

"This goal is moderately important to me personally. Organizing contact information makes calling on clients easier. It's also personally satisfying to me. This goal has low professional importance, though. My boss doesn't care how well I maintain my contact database."

Perform at least ten sales presentations to potential new clients within 120 days.

"This goal has a low level of personal importance for me. I don't enjoy giving presentations to potential clients. I prefer working with established accounts. However, this goal has high professional importance. I'm evaluated on the number of presentations I give."

Prepare a training presentation to help new customers use the company's identification system effectively.

"This goal has a high level of personal importance for me. I like to teach new clients how to make the most of our company's products. This goal also has a high level of professional importance. My boss expects me to train new clients and win their trust."

The priority you assign to a goal should be determined by the availability of resources you can apply to achieving it. There are two factors to consider about resource availability: resource readiness and resource urgency.

See the two factors to consider about resource availability to learn more about them.

Resource readiness

Resource readiness is the amount of time, money, materials, or knowledge ready to be applied. You're able to act more quickly when resources are available.

Resource urgency

The urgency of resources is how quickly resources must be used. If a deadline is approaching or a key team member will soon become unavailable, urgency is high.

Warren, the sales representative for the identification systems company, evaluated the readiness and urgency of resources he could apply to his three goals.

See each of the goals to learn how they differ in the resources Warren can apply.

Update customer contact information in company sales database.

"This goal has a low level of resource readiness. I need at least one full day to perform this task, but my schedule is full. The urgency to perform this task is low. I can afford to postpone organizing my client contact information. There's no deadline for getting it done."

Perform at least ten sales presentations to potential clients within 120 days.

"This goal has a very low level of resource readiness. I don't have the required knowledge to perform these presentations. The person who can help me is out of town for a month. However, the urgency to complete this goal is growing. The time to my deadline is growing short."

Prepare training presentation to help new customers use the company's identification system effectively.

"This goal has a high level of resource readiness. I have the time I need to work on this task and a training specialist has been assigned to me. The urgency for this goal is moderate. I may have plenty of time, but the training specialist won't be available after next week."

Question

Gail has set a goal to obtain a certification in computer network security. However, this is only one of several goals she hopes to achieve within the next year. Which are factors she should consider to help her prioritize this goal?

Options:

1. Understanding network security is only moderately important to me personally.

2. A certification in network security would make me much more valuable to my company.

3. I don't have much free time in my schedule. I don't know how I'll find time to take network security courses.

4. My goal is to complete a network security certification within the next year. To meet that goal, I'll need to start taking courses immediately.

5. Computer networking is a boring subject. I probably won't enjoy taking the classes.

Answer:

Gail should prioritize this goal using each of the four factors: personal value, professional value, resource readiness, and resource urgency. If there are other factors that make this goal urgent, she should think about that separately.

Option 1: This is a correct choice. The personal value of achieving this goal is one of the factors Gail should consider to prioritize this goal. This goal is only moderately important to Gail, so it would have a moderate personal value.

Option 2: This is a correct choice. The professional value of this goal is a factor Gail should consider. Completing a certification course would make her a more valuable employee to her company, so this goal has a high professional value.

Option 3: This is a correct option. The availability of resources to achieve a goal is a factor Gail should consider. If Gail doesn't have free time to devote to her goal, resource readiness is low.

Option 4: This is a correct option. A special urgency to act on this goal is a factor Gail should use to prioritize this goal among her other goals. The urgency to apply available resources is a factor Gail must consider.

Option 5: This is not a correct choice. Gail should determine whether the result of taking the classes is important, not whether she'll enjoy the process of achieving her goal.

To prioritize a set of goals, you must weigh the importance and resource availability to be applied for each one. Then compare each goal to all the others.

First, rate each goal on a scale of 1 to 5 for personal importance and professional importance. Assign a value of

1 to goals with relatively low importance. Assign a value of 5 to very important goals.

Add the values for personal importance and professional importance together to obtain a total value for the importance of each goal.

Calculate an importance value for all of the goals that must be prioritized. The results will all fall between 2 for the least important goals and 10 for the most important goals.

Perform the same process for resource readiness and resource urgency. Assign a value between 1 and 5 for each criterion.

Assign low values to goals for which resources aren't readily available and for which urgency is low. Assign high values to goals where plenty of resources are readily available and the urgency to act is high. Add the two values together.

Calculate a resource availability value for all of the goals to be prioritized. The total for each goal will fall between 2 for the goals with the lowest resource availability and 10 for the goals with the highest resource availability.

Plot the values for each goal on a priorities matrix. The vertical scale represents the importance. The horizontal scale represents the resource availability.

The position of the goals on the priorities matrix gives you an indication of the priority you should set for each one. Divide the matrix into four zones as shown. Place the dividing lines between zones 5 and 6 on both the vertical and horizontal scales.

Check each zone in the matrix to learn how goals in that zone should be prioritized.

Zone 2

Goals in zone 2 can be delayed until later but must be watched carefully. These goals have a high level of importance, but resources aren't available or there isn't an urgent need to act. A change in resource availability could raise the priority of these goals.

Zone 1

Goals that fall in zone 1 are top priorities. They have a high level of importance and resources are available. You should act immediately to achieve these goals.

Zone 4

Goals in zone 4 aren't important and resources aren't available. You may consider abandoning these goals.

Zone 3

Goals in zone 3 should be reconsidered or reformulated. Although resources are available, these goals don't have a high level of importance. Until they become more meaningful, there's no hurry to act on these goals.

Warren, the account representative, created a list of goals he wanted to pursue. His list is shown above.

He rated each of his goals for resource readiness and for urgency. He added the ratings together to obtain a total rating for resource availability.

Warren rated each goal for personal and professional importance. He added the ratings for each goal together to obtain an overall importance rating.

Warren used a priorities matrix to prioritize his goals. He used the resource availability rating and the importance rating to place a data point for each goal on the matrix. Warren used the location of the data points to determine the priority of each goal.

Check the data points in the priorities matrix to learn how Warren rated each of his goals and the priorities he set as a result.

3

This data point represents Warren's goal to prepare training for new clients. He rated this goal 7 for resource availability and 9 for importance. The data point for this goal is in zone 1, so Warren should make it a top priority.

2

This data point represents Warren's goal to perform ten new sales presentations. This goal has a resource availability rating of 4 and an importance rating of 7. This data point is in zone 2. Warren can delay acting on this goal, but he should watch for changes.

5

This data point represents Warren's goal to receive mentoring. He gave this goal a total resource availability rating of 5 and an importance rating of 7, so it falls in zone 2. Warren can delay acting on this goal, but he should watch for changes.

4

This data point represents Warren's goal to perform a return-on-investment analysis. He gave this goal a rating of 7 for resource availability and a rating of 8 for importance. The data point is in zone 1, so Warren should make this goal a top priority.

1

This data point represents Warren's goal to organize his client contact file. He gave this goal a rating of 4 for resource availability and a rating of 4 for importance. Because the data point for this goal is in zone 4, Warren should consider abandoning it.

When Warren plotted his goals on a priorities matrix, the goals that were most important and most achievable became apparent. He applied his immediate efforts to achieving those goals.

However, he didn't neglect the rest. He made conscious decisions about delaying, reconsidering, or abandoning the others.

Case Study: Question 1 of 3
Scenario

Todd is a project manager for a civil engineering firm. Todd set the following goals for the coming year: -- Develop a list of requirements for a proposed software application.

--Update the project schedule for a bridge construction project.

--Prepare a schedule proposal for a water pipeline project.

--Calculate costs and benefits of quality assurance standards.

--Seek mentoring on ways to lead virtual teams scattered among several cities.

Answer the questions in order.

Question:

Todd rated his goals using four criteria. Access the learning aid Todd's Goals to learn about his ratings. Todd used the ratings to plot three goals on a priorities matrix. Match the correct data point to each of Todd's goals. One data point has no match.

Options:
A. data point C
B. data point H
C. data point G

D. data point A

Targets:

1. Develop a list of requirements for a software application.
2. Prepare a schedule proposal for a water pipeline project.
3. Seek mentoring on ways to lead virtual teams.

Answer:

You're not using Todd's ratings correctly to calculate the placement of each goal on the matrix.

This goal should be plotted as data point G. Todd ranked the resource availability as an 8 and the importance of the goal as an 8. The proper coordinates for this goal are (8, 8).

The pipeline project should be plotted at data point C. The resource availability for this goal was rated 5 and the importance was rated 7. Therefore, the proper coordinates are (5, 7).

Todd's goal to seek mentoring should be plotted at data point A. He rated the resource availability on this goal as 4 and the importance of this goal as 8. The correct coordinates are (4, 8).

Case Study: Question 2 of 3

Todd plotted the remaining two goals to the priorities matrix.

Match the correct data point to each of Todd's goals. Two data points have no match.

Options:

A. data point D
B. data point F
C. data point B
D. data point E

Targets:
1. Calculate costs and benefits of quality assurance standards.
2. Update the schedule for a bridge construction project.

Answer:
The resource pressure for each goal is the sum of resource availability and resource urgency. This total is the coordinate on the horizontal scale. The sum of personal and professional importance is the coordinate on the vertical scale.

This goal should be plotted at data point F. Todd rated the resource pressure for this goal at 7 and the importance of the goal at 5. The correct coordinates are (7, 5).

Todd should plot this goal at data point E. He rated the resource pressure at 7 and the importance of the goal at 6. The coordinates for this goal are (7, 6).

Case Study: Question 3 of 3
After he plotted all of his goals on the priorities matrix, Todd assigned priority levels to his goals.

Match the priority levels to one or more of Todd's goals. Not all priority levels may have a match.

Options:
A. Act immediately.
B. Delay and monitor this goal for changes.
C. Reconsider this goal.
D. Consider abandoning this goal.

Targets:
1. Develop a list of requirements for a software application.
2. Update the schedule for a bridge construction project.

3. Prepare a schedule proposal for a water pipeline project.

4. Calculate costs and benefits of quality assurance standards.

5. Seek mentoring on ways to lead virtual teams.

Answer:

Todd should act immediately on important goals for which resources are available. He should watch for changing conditions on important goals where resources are scarce. Goals with low importance should be reconsidered or dropped.

Todd should act immediately on this goal. It has a high level of importance. Resources to work toward this goal are available and the urgency to use those resources is high.

Todd should act immediately to achieve this goal. This goal has a high degree of professional importance and resources are readily available.

Todd should monitor this goal for changes. Although this goal has a high degree of personal importance for Todd, the urgency to use the available resources is currently very low.

Todd should reconsider this goal. Although resources are available, it has a low degree of importance. He should decide whether it's worth pursuing or reformulate it so it becomes more important.

Todd should monitor this goal for changes. This goal has a very high degree of personal importance and a moderate degree of professional importance. However, resources to pursue this goal aren't available.

When Todd plotted his goals to a priorities matrix, he recognized that his software requirements goal and his bridge project update goal should be his top priorities.

The ratings Todd applied to determine his priorities were entirely subjective. If the priorities don't seem appropriate, Todd may reconsider some of his ratings.

Working toward several goals at once doesn't have to be an impossible juggling act. It's just a matter of prioritizing action on the most important and achievable goals.

STRATEGIES FOR SETTING ALTERNATIVE GOALS

Strategies for setting alternative goals

There will be times when you can't achieve some of your goals. That's when it's time to consider alternative goals.

You don't have to give up on a goal just because it doesn't work out the way you expected. Persistence will result in success. You can set an alternative goal using one of these three strategies:
- breaking out smaller objectives,
- reassessing priorities,
- seeking a different path to the destination.

The first strategy for setting alternative goals is breaking out smaller objectives. When a larger objective can't be obtained within the standard you've set, breaking out a smaller objective allows you to be partially successful.

To break out a smaller objective, see if there's a portion of your original goal that can be achieved separately. Narrow the effect of your goal on fewer people or events.

You can always address the remainder of your original goal later.

Vicki is a broker for a financial services firm. She set a goal to increase her sales by 12 percent. Her original strategy was to find 20 new clients by the end of the year. Her original goal now seems too challenging, so Vicki is considering alternative goals.

See each method of breaking out a smaller goal from an original goal to learn more about how Vicki can go about doing this.

Smaller goal

Vicki can limit her goal to a single product line, like life insurance or retirement accounts. Achieving a 12 percent increase in a limited area will be a partial success.

New goal

Vicki can create a new goal to increase her sales in other product lines later. That will allow her to achieve her original goal.

The second strategy for setting alternative goals is reassessing priorities. Another look at the importance and resources associated with a goal may reveal changes in either or both elements of the goal's priority.

Don't be afraid to postpone dealing with one goal in order to pursue a goal that has become more important. You can return to your original goal later if changing conditions make it important again.

Vicki, the financial services company broker, had set a goal to receive mentoring on closing sales from her sales team leader.

However, her sales team leader couldn't make time to provide the training. Vicki reassessed the priority of receiving mentoring.

The resources Vicki needed to develop her sales closing skills weren't available.

She decided she could delay working on that skill.

With her sales team leader's advice, she decided to make developing her knowledge of the company's products a higher priority.

The third strategy for setting alternative goals is choosing a different path. There's more than one way to reach most destinations. If you can't develop or improve skills through education, you can choose on- the-job experience, or find a mentor instead.

You can improve profitability by increasing sales or by reducing costs. You can save time by doing work more quickly or by eliminating unnecessary work. Choosing a different path allows you to take an alternate route to your objective.

Vicki could choose to take a different path to achieve her goal of a 12 percent sales increase. See each potential path to learn more about it.

New customers

Vicki's original strategy was to find 20 new clients. Her sales to new clients would provide the increase in sales to achieve her goal.

Existing customers

Instead of seeking 20 new clients, Vicki chose to focus on her existing clients. She set up meetings with her ten largest clients to show them additional products her company offers.

There are a couple of common strategies you shouldn't use when you need an alternative goal. Relaxing the standard for your goal isn't a good strategy. Extending your deadline or reducing the amount of change you expect to achieve is just lowering the standard for success, not setting an alternative goal.

Ignoring the conditions on your original goal is also not a good strategy. Conditions limit how you go about achieving a goal to prevent unwanted or unexpected results. Ignoring them may make achieving your goal more costly.

Question

Gail set a goal to complete all the required courses for a certification in computer network security within a year without taking time off from work. Now Gail must reconsider her goal because she needs to devote more time to taking care of an ailing relative. Select examples of appropriate strategies for Gail to use to set an alternative goal.

Options:

1. Complete the courses she can apply to her job immediately and complete the remaining courses at another time.

2. Discuss with her supervisor whether a network security certification is the best way for her to become more valuable to the company.

3. Investigate whether there's a way to gain experience in computer network security from on-the-job experience.

4. Decide whether to change her self-imposed deadline from one year to two years.

5. Discuss with her supervisor whether she can take a leave of absence to complete the most difficult course.

Answer:

Breaking out a smaller objective, reassessing priorities, and choosing an alternative path are appropriate ways to set alternative goals. The other options are simply ways of lowering standards or compromising conditions.

Option 1: This is a correct option. Gail is breaking her original objective--earn a certification in computer network security--into two objectives. As an alternative to her original goal, she can complete one of the new objectives immediately.

Option 2: This is a correct choice. If Gail and her supervisor can identify development goals that are more valuable or more urgent, Gail may shift her priorities to emphasize another goal.

Option 3: This is a correct option. Choosing another path to reach her original objective is a way to set an alternative goal. Developing her skills through on-the-job experience is an alternative path to taking courses.

Option 4: This is not a correct choice. Relaxing the deadline changes the standards component of Gail's original goal. This is just lowering the standard for success, not setting an alternative goal.

Option 5: This is not a correct choice. This option changes the conditions component of Gail's original goal. A change in conditions may alter the resources required to achieve a goal.

Goals should be reassessed and reworked continuously. Knowing how to set alternative goals gives you a way to try, try again if at first you don't succeed.

CREATING A POSITIVE ATTITUDE

Creating a Positive Attitude

Have you ever noticed how some people can see something good in every situation? One of the best ways to do this is to alter the way you look at the situations you find yourself in. Positive people always look at things from a positive perspective.

You may be lucky enough to have a "sunny disposition," but most people find themselves looking at the negative side of situations at some point. If you can look at what happens to you from a positive perspective, then you can deal with situations positively.

The locus of control refers to what individuals believe is the controlling force behind the events that happen to them. It can be described as either internal or external. Individuals with an internal locus of control are likely to believe that events result from their own behaviors and actions.

How you think about something influences how you feel about it. Your feelings then influence how you behave in response. If your internal response to the events that happen to you is rational, then you can avoid the negative side effects that result from unrealistic or unfounded expectations and doubts. But what is the difference between rational and irrational internal responses?

John W. Gardner, the former Secretary of Health, Education, and Welfare, once said, "We are continually faced with a series of great opportunities brilliantly disguised as insoluble problems."

The idea that opportunities are disguised as problems demonstrates how, by looking at a situation in a different way, you can see new possibilities.

It's one thing to try to develop a positive perspective on the things that happen to you, but how will you cope when faced with people and situations that make you feel negative?

Coping starts with taking action to catch yourself before negative feelings take over. Do things that help you minimize your negativity, and if necessary, challenge difficult people and situations so that you can sustain a positive outlook.

Do you ever hear a little voice inside your head, criticizing and undermining you? The language that voice uses reflects the nature of your thoughts and beliefs. If you can change it to a supportive voice, you'll be on the way to having a positive attitude. The voice inside your head can direct the way you think and behave.

You can apply four simple techniques to help you. You may find that you need to use all four techniques, or you might find that one of them works well for you. The techniques are examining the evidence, befriending yourself, putting things in context, and looking for the positive. Underpinning all of these techniques is a need to challenge your negative thinking.

Unfortunately, you don't have control over what people say to you--but you do have control over how you respond. One of the most difficult times to respond to someone is when you are being criticized, particularly when that criticism does not appear to be constructive or even justified.

Feeling out of control is one of the most common triggers for negative thinking. If you feel as if you can't influence what happens to you, then you begin to lack confidence and believe the worst is inevitable.

CHANGING PERSPECTIVE

Changing perspective

Have you ever noticed how some people can see something good in every situation? One of the best ways to do this is to alter the way you look at the situations you find yourself in. Positive people always look at things from a positive perspective.

You may be lucky enough to have a "sunny disposition," but most people find themselves looking at the negative side of situations at some point. If you can look at what happens to you from a positive perspective, then you can deal with situations positively.

Changing your perspective from negative to positive can benefit you by:
- enabling you to take control of what happens to you,
- letting you examine your reactions so that you don't overreact to situations,
- allowing you to think of creative ways to deal with negative situations that you face.

Developing a positive attitude means taking a positive stance when faced with a situation, instead of withdrawing or focusing on the negative aspects of a situation.

Your ability to do this is governed by your perspective on a situation. If you can look at things from a positive standpoint instead of a negative one, you can take positive steps to deal with the issues you face.

Before you change your perspective, you need to understand what your current perspective is.

The best way to do this is to consider three aspects of any situation: what or who you believe to be in control of the situation, the extent to which your reactions are rational, and whether you focus on the negative or positive aspects of a situation.

This lesson helps you to understand what your perspective is, how it impacts your reactions, and how you can change your perspective so that you can develop a positive attitude.

Question

How can changing your perspective benefit you in dealing positively with situations?

Options:

1. I'll be able to devise creative solutions to the problems that I face.

2. I'll be able to ensure that I don't overreact to situations.

3. I'll be able to make sure that nothing bad ever happens.

4. I'll be able to take control over what happens to me.

5. I'll be able to avoid taking responsibility for my mistakes.

Answer:

Option 1: This option is correct. By developing a positive perspective you'll be able to look at the situations you face and find creative ways to deal with them.

Option 2: This option is correct. By developing a positive perspective you'll be able to examine your reactions to situations and ensure that your reactions are appropriate and proportionate.

Option 3: This option is incorrect. Unfortunately, however positive your attitude, you can't guarantee things will always go well.

Option 4: This option is correct. By developing a positive perspective you'll be able to take control of what is happening to you instead of allowing yourself to be overwhelmed by events.

Option 5: This option is incorrect. Unfortunately, however positive your attitude, you can't avoid taking responsibility for mistakes that you've made.

"Always look on the bright side" may sound like stereotyped advice from someone who doesn't understand how difficult your situation is.

But if you do change your perspective to be positive, then you'll find that you can avoid overreacting to the situations that you face, take control of what happens to you, and find creative ways of dealing with adversity.

INTERNAL AND EXTERNAL LOCI OF CONTROL

Internal and external loci of control

Who is in control of your life? The locus of control concept was proposed by the psychologist Julian Rotter in 1966.

The locus of control refers to what individuals believe is the controlling force behind the events that happen to them. It can be described as either internal or external.

Individuals with an internal locus of control are likely to believe that events result from their own behaviors and actions.

See each aspect to find out how having an internal locus of control can affect your attitude.

Responsibility

Individuals with an internal locus of control are willing to take responsibility for their own actions, and for what happens to them.

Positive attitude

Doing Business Professionally

Individuals with an internal locus of control generally have a positive attitude because they feel they can have an impact on their own lives.

Follow along as Danny, an account executive, explains what has happened to him at work over the past few weeks.

I knew my boss was right when she criticized my handling of the Adams account in my appraisal. I had the opportunity to win the business, but I just didn't go that extra mile.

If I worked a little harder, I would have gotten the account and met my targets for the month. I'll know better next time.

I know that in the long term, I'll be able to meet my targets and my boss will respect the work that I've put in. The only person who can help me succeed is me, so I need to focus hard and get the job done.

Individuals with an external locus of control believe that chance, luck, or powerful people determine events.

Individuals with an external locus of control may have a tendency to distance themselves from events and their consequences, blaming others, fate, or the situation for what is happening, instead of taking responsibility for themselves.

As a result, individuals with an external locus of control often fail to have positive attitudes because they feel paralyzed and unable to act to change what is happening to them.

Patty is a colleague of Danny's, and she has also recently had an appraisal with her boss. Follow along as Patty describes what has happened to her.

My boss just doesn't understand how hard I'm working. If she doesn't realize how much effort I'm putting in, then there's nothing I can do.

It's not my fault if the customers don't want to buy; it's just one of those things. There's nothing I can do about it.

If I had the right breaks, I'd easily meet my targets. It's just a matter of being in the right place at the right time. One day I'll have some luck--then my boss will realize what a great account executive I am.

Danny and Patty reacted very differently to their appraisals. Why was that? See each person to find out more.

Patty

Patty has a high external locus of control. She believes that luck will help her achieve her targets and that what her customers decide to do is outside of her control. She distances herself from her failures and doesn't take responsibility for her actions.

Danny

Danny has a high internal locus of control. He believes he's responsible for what happens to him, and as a result, he feels he can improve his performance and achieve his targets in the future.

Awareness of your locus of control can help you develop a positive attitude.

If your locus of control is external, you need to take steps to take responsibility for what happens to you, and to believe that you can positively influence your own destiny.

If you have an internal locus of control, you take responsibility for your actions; however, it may also be good to remind yourself that sometimes it's important to take external factors into account.

Question

Some people feel that what happens to them is a matter of fate, and others believe that they can influence events as a result of their actions. Match these loci of control to one or more of these examples.

Options:

A. internal locus of control
B. external locus of control

Targets:

1. I've been promoted because I worked hard.
2. I gave the interview a good shot, but I guess I could have done more research.
3. I was promoted because my boss likes me, not because I'm good at my job.
4. I worked hard. I can't help it if they don't like me.
5. I only passed the exam because I got lucky with the questions.

Answer:

Individuals who have an internal locus of control take responsibility for their actions, whereas those with an external locus of control tend to blame or credit fate or other people for successes or failures.

This is an example of someone with an internal locus of control. This person believes his success is the result of his own actions.

This is an example of someone with an internal locus of control. This person believes that if she'd been more prepared for her interview, it would have gone better. This admission involves taking responsibility for her actions.

This is an example of someone with an external locus of control. This person believes that his success is the result of external factors--in this case, the fact that his boss likes him.

This is an example of someone with an external locus of control. This person believes his failure is the result of someone else's attitude toward him. He is blaming external factors for his failure.

This is an example of someone with an external locus of control. This person believes her success didn't result from hard work, but from being "lucky" with the questions--an external factor.

The novelist John Oliver Hobbes once said, "Men heap together the mistakes of their lives, and create a monster they call destiny."

Don't let an external locus of control become the monster that stops you from achieving what you're capable of. Challenge your perspective on what happens to you, and take action to develop a more positive outlook.

A RATIONAL RESPONSE TO A SEQUENCE OF EVENTS

A rational response to a sequence of events

In the Shakespeare play Hamlet, the Prince of Denmark said:

"There's nothing either good or bad, but thinking makes it so."

How you think about something influences how you feel about it. Your feelings then influence how you behave in response.

If your internal response to the events that happen to you is rational, then you can avoid the negative side effects that result from unrealistic or unfounded expectations and doubts. But what is the difference between rational and irrational internal responses?

See the responses to find out more.

Rational

Rational perceptions are those that are based on realistic beliefs about events. In most cases, the most likely explanation for events is the true explanation.

Irrational

Irrational perceptions are those based on unrealistic beliefs about events. People aren't usually devious and underhanded; believing so is unrealistic and irrational.

Albert Ellis, a pioneer of cognitive therapy, devised the ABC model for emotional disturbance and change.

The ABC model comprises three distinct elements:
- A stands for an actual event and represents what happens to you.
- B stands for a belief about what happened.
- C stands for the consequences of the event on mood and behavior.

Harry is the supervisor of a telephone customer service team. Harry needs to change the office layout to make space for two new employees and some new printing and photocopying equipment, and to comply with his organization's new guidelines for workspaces.

See each person to find out what choices Harry makes about who should be located where, and why.

Jason

Jason is relatively new to the team, so Harry decides to place Jason's desk close to his office and right next to Arthur, one of the most experienced members of the team. This way, Jason can easily ask for help from either Arthur or Harry whenever he needs it.

Joan

Joan acts as Harry's personal assistant and also deals with customers. Harry locates Joan's desk just outside his office and close to the printing and photocopying equipment. This way, she can contact Harry easily, but she also has access to the equipment she needs.

Lillian

Doing Business Professionally

Lillian is one of three technical specialists who deal with technical queries. Harry decides to locate one technical specialist within each group of workspaces so that technical advice is always available to other employees. As a result, Lillian is relocated to a desk next to the window.

Arthur

Arthur is the most experienced member of the team, and he often mentors new employees. Harry relocates Arthur from his isolated workspace next to the window to a new workspace close to his office. From here, Arthur can better support the new hires.

See each person to find out how Harry's team members have responded.

Jason

Jason believes his desk has been located between Harry and Arthur because he isn't trusted, and so he leaves the meeting angry when the office layout is revealed.

Joan

Joan understands that, because of her dual role as Harry's personal assistant and customer service assistant, she needs to be close to Harry and the printing and photocopying equipment. She doesn't particularly like her new workspace, but she isn't upset to have been moved.

Lillian

Although Lillian is pleased to be next to the window, she believes Harry deliberately moved her away from her friends on the technical team because she talks to them too much, and so she reacts by sulking.

Arthur

Arthur knows his old location was isolated, but he really liked being by the window. Last week, Arthur disagreed with Harry about how to deal with a difficult client, and now he feels as though Harry is punishing him by moving him.

Jason, Arthur, and Lillian all responded irrationally to the office layout because they believed Harry's motives were personal, unfair, or prejudiced.

In fact, if they had thought about what Harry was trying to achieve, they would each have seen that Harry was just trying to make the team work as effectively as possible--and their reactions would have been rational.

Joan responded rationally. She understood why Harry needed to make the changes to the office layout, so she was the only team member able to have a positive attitude about the changes.

Question

Your boss has been out of the office for a while. After a team meeting, he asks if you can stay to discuss things.

Which of these are rational responses to your manager's request?

Options:

1. He's going to give me a formal warning about my input into the meeting.

2. He wants to discuss something that isn't relevant to the other meeting attendees.

3. He's going to fire me.

4. He wants to catch up because we haven't spoken for a while.

5. He's going to tell me I've been passed over for promotion.

Answer:

Option 1: This option is incorrect. A rational response is based on realistic beliefs about events. It is unlikely your boss would give a formal warning about input to a meeting, and if this was the case, it would be done in a formal meeting.

Option 2: This option is correct. A rational response is based on realistic beliefs about events. It's realistic to believe that if your boss asks to speak to you after the meeting, it may well be to discuss something that isn't relevant to the other attendees.

Option 3: This option is incorrect. A rational response is based on realistic beliefs about events. In the majority of organizations, your boss would have to implement formal procedures to fire you; he wouldn't simply fire you at the end of a meeting.

Option 4: This option is correct. A rational response is based on realistic beliefs about events. If you haven't seen each other for a while, one of the best explanations for his wanting to talk to you is the need to catch up.

Option 5: This option is incorrect. A rational response is based on realistic beliefs about events. Is after a meeting really the right time to talk about a promotion? You should always consider the most likely explanation for an event, not the most dramatic.

Oftentimes, your negative feelings about what happens to you are a direct result of the way you perceive events. Stand back, try not to take things personally, and see what happens.

Reacting rationally to the events you encounter is a good way to develop a positive attitude.

POSITIVE FRAMES

Positive frames

John W. Gardner, the former Secretary of Health, Education, and Welfare, once said, "We are continually faced with a series of great opportunities brilliantly disguised as insoluble problems."

The idea that opportunities are disguised as problems demonstrates how, by looking at a situation in a different way, you can see new possibilities.

Creating new perspectives, or frames, can help you think beyond your own experiences and look at things in new and more positive ways.

But what kind of perspectives should you consider?

The key to using frames is to focus on the positive perspectives, not the negative ones. There are four main pairs of frames:
- problem and learning,
- detail and overall,
- personal and team,
- conflict and negotiation

The problem frame is a negative frame in which every issue is seen as a problem. Conversely, the learning frame is a positive frame in which everything is seen as a learning opportunity.

By switching your perspective from seeing negative problems to seeing positive learning opportunities, you can begin to see the good in situations that, at first glance, appear to be disastrous.

Danny and Patty are account executives for a large public relations firm. They recently worked on a project for a pharmaceutical company. Unfortunately, the firm missed a few key deadlines, and the client was angry.

See each person for examples of viewing this situation through the problem frame and the learning frame.

Danny

Danny used the situation to revise his project plan template so key deadlines were tracked. He also created a new procedure for managing suppliers and contracts.

Patty

Patty saw the situation as hopeless. She assumed the relationship with the client had been irrevocably broken and that she would be removed from the account.

The detail and overall pair of frames is useful when you need to be able to step back from a situation, and view it from a broader perspective. In the detail frame, the focus is on a single element of an issue, whereas in the overall frame, the focus is on an entire issue, rather than one element.

Review the situations and solutions to find out how Tim, a project manager, and Mary, a chef, each switched from the detail frame to the overall frame to look at events in a positive way.

Tim's Detail

"I was panicking because our quality assurance procedures were quite cumbersome, and following them would mean the project wouldn't be completed on time."

Tim's Overall

"Then I stepped back and analyzed the project as a whole. I realized that simply deleting a couple of steps from the quality assurance process would allow us to meet our deadline without affecting the entire project."

Mary's Detail

"I was catering a wedding reception. I wanted to use Scottish oysters, but I could only get French ones. It worried me because I think the Scottish oysters are better quality."

Mary's Overall

"It suddenly occurred to me that my opinion didn't matter. The guests wouldn't care whether I served Scottish or French oysters; they would be focused on enjoying the happy occasion."

The personal and team frame pair can be very useful when used together with the detail and overall frames.

- In the personal frame, an individual focuses only on what is happening to him instead of how events impact on others, the project, or the organization as a whole.
- In the team frame, the individual focuses on how events affect the team or organization as a whole rather than how they affect him.

Tim and Mary have both found that by switching from the personal to the team frame, they have been able to react more positively to what is happening to them. Specifically, using these frames can help you to remove yourself from the center of a situation and see what is really happening.

Select each person to find out how Tim and Mary switched from the personal frame to the team frame so they now look at events in a positive way.

Tim

"I'd finished my deadline and was looking forward to a couple of easy workdays before the next project hit. Then I realized that other team members needed help finishing their tasks or we would miss the project deadline, so I volunteered to pitch in."

Mary

"With the wedding only a week away, I felt like all the pressure was on me, and I was being pretty difficult to work with. Then I recognized that we were all feeling the pressure. I resolved to shift my focus to the wedding and what we had to do to make it successful."

The final pair of frames, conflict and negotiation, is also linked closely to the other pairs of frames. This is because the conflict frame is a negative frame in which the focus of the issue is disagreement and winning, rather than resolution and compromise.

This often means that personal issues overshadow what is good for the team or the organization.

The negotiation frame is a positive frame in which the focus is on conflict resolution and compromise.

Switching to this frame often results in a refocusing on the positive overall and team frames.

Oliver and his colleague Jim can't agree on the best way to approach a technical problem on their building project. Follow along as they discuss what is happening.

Oliver: As I see it, we can fix this if your guys dig another foot down so that we can add more concrete. We could add steelwork but that would be too costly. You'll just have to do it.

Jim: Well, we wouldn't have this problem if you'd specified the concrete properly. I don't see why my team should have to work longer just because you made an error in your calculations.

Jim says defensively.

Oliver: OK. This is getting us nowhere. We're not going to agree on why we're in this position, but what we can agree on is that we have to move forward. How can we work together?

Oliver acknowledges.

Jim: I guess we could compromise. I can get my team to start digging now, and we'll see how far we get by close of business. Then we can look again.

Jim compromises.

Reframing or looking at things from positive perspectives will enable you to overcome your negative thoughts and feelings. It will also help you discover new ways of approaching situations that might have overwhelmed you in the past.

Question

Positive reframing is an effective technique for looking for the best in situations.

Match each positive frame with its corresponding example.

Options:
A. learning
B. overall
C. team

D. negotiation

Targets:

1. Carmen saw that her car breaking down was an opportunity to look into replacing it.

2. Bradley saw that checking all line items did not have an effect on the whole project.

3. Jill stopped thinking people were picking on her and offered to help her coworkers.

4. Miles and Carmen agreed that each of their teams would compromise on a solution.

Answer:

This is an example of positively reframing from the problem frame to the learning frame by seeing the good in situations that, at first glance, appear to be disastrous--in this case, considering getting a new car.

This is an example of positively reframing from the detail frame to the overall frame by thinking about the project as a whole instead of focusing on the details of a specific process.

This is an example of positively reframing from the personal frame to the team frame by thinking about what is good for the team instead of what is good for the individual.

This is an example of positively reframing from the conflict frame to the negotiation frame by focusing on resolution and compromise instead of disagreement and winning.

Where some people see problems, others see opportunities.

Looking at situations from a positive perspective is a good way of turning your problems into opportunities, and a way of making sure that you get the best out of the situations you face.

CHANGING COPING SKILLS TO REACT POSITIVELY TO SITUATIONS

Changing coping skills to react positively to situations

It's one thing to try to develop a positive perspective on the things that happen to you, but how will you cope when faced with people and situations that make you feel negative?

Coping starts with taking action to catch yourself before negative feelings take over.

Do things that help you minimize your negativity, and if necessary, challenge difficult people and situations so that you can sustain a positive outlook.

Changing your coping skills to react positively to situations can help you:
- base your reactions on facts,
- improve your performance,
- set boundaries and avoid feelings of frustration and being taken advantage of.

Patty works as an account executive and has a reputation for being negative. Recently, however, Patty has been working hard to change her coping skills so that she can handle negative situations better.

Select the stages to find out how Patty felt before she changed her coping skills, and how she has benefited as a result of her efforts.

Before

"Looking back to my appraisal, I thought my boss was criticizing me because she didn't like me, and I felt that I was being given the most difficult clients and the least interesting jobs deliberately. I felt so miserable because I was negative about everything."

After

"I get the clients I get because that's just how things work out--I was overreacting before. I've used the feedback I've been given to improve my performance, and I realize that I'm not being taken advantage of--we're all treated equally. I feel much more positive now."

Question

What benefits will you realize by changing your coping skills to react positively to situations?

Options:

1. I'll be able to base my reactions to situations on what is actually happening.

2. I'll be able to improve my performance.

3. I'll be able to set boundaries and avoid being taken advantage of.

4. I'll be able to ensure that I don't get angry or upset when other people behave unreasonably.

5. I'll be able to avoid doing things that I don't want to do.

Answer:

Option 1: This option is correct. By changing your coping skills, you'll be able to base your reactions to situations and people on facts, and you won't overreact.

Option 2: This option is correct. By developing a positive perspective, you'll be able to improve your performance as a result of making use of the feedback you receive.

Option 3: This option is correct. By developing a positive perspective, you'll be able to stop feeling as if you're being taken advantage of because you'll be able to set boundaries.

Option 4: This option is incorrect. Unfortunately, however good your coping skills are, you may still find yourself feeling hurt or angry as a result of other people's actions.

Option 5: This option is incorrect. Setting boundaries doesn't enable you to opt out of activities you don't like. Changing your coping skills will help you to deal with these activities, not avoid them altogether.

Comic artist Tom K. Ryan once said "I will cope with adversity in my traditional manner... sulking and nausea."

A better strategy is to turn adversity to your benefit by developing techniques to cope and overcome the problems you face. As a result, you'll benefit from the positive outcomes that result from a positive attitude.

TECHNIQUES USED TO CHALLENGE NEGATIVE THINKING

Techniques used to challenge negative thinking

Do you ever hear a little voice inside your head, criticizing and undermining you? The language that voice uses reflects the nature of your thoughts and beliefs.

If you can change it to a supportive voice, you'll be on the way to having a positive attitude. The voice inside your head can direct the way you think and behave.

See each type to find out how negative and positive thinking can affect you.

Negative thinking

Negative thinking undermines you and makes you believe that you can't succeed.

Positive thinking

Positive thinking gives you the confidence to take up new challenges and to believe that you can succeed.

By changing negative thoughts to positive ones, you'll find that you can manage your responses to events, and react more rationally.

Broadly speaking, there are five distinct areas of negative thoughts that need to be overcome. See each of the items below to find out more about these areas of negative thoughts:

focusing on the negative

Focusing on the negative involves selecting a single negative aspect of an experience and focusing entirely on that. Focusing on the negative can also involve dismissing and devaluing positive experiences by putting any successes down to luck.

all or nothing thinking

All or nothing thinking involves looking at things in black and white terms--everything was good or everything was bad. Often, all or nothing thinking will involve misreading people's reactions or overdramatizing the importance of a minor problem.

overgeneralization and labeling

When you engage in overgeneralization, you see a single negative event as a never-ending pattern of defeat. In its most extreme form, it involves attaching a negative label, such as idiot or failure, to yourself or others.

jumping to conclusions

Jumping to conclusions is also known as "mind reading" and "fortune-telling," and it involves imagining unrealistic negative outcomes or consequences of an event.

blame

Blame happens when you hold someone or something else entirely responsible for an event. Oftentimes, it involves an "I told you so" attitude.

Tim is a project manager who has managed the design of a major line of toys. Tim has just presented his team's designs to the client, and although the client liked most of the ideas, they requested a minor change to one of the toy's colors.

See the thought processes to find out how Tim reacted internally.

Negative Focus

"How could we have been so off on that color? It isn't what they wanted; they'd asked for a different shade of blue. We were lucky they liked the designs."

All or Nothing

"What a disaster. The color was wrong, so I guess it's back to the drawing board. We spent so much time on this project, and they hated it."

The meeting with the client wasn't Tim's only negative experience. There have been problems with some of the suppliers, and the marketing department has just told him they're having difficulty booking media space for the launch. Can things get any worse for Tim?

See each type of negative thought Tim is having to learn more.

Overgeneralization and Labeling

"I'm such an idiot. This always happens to me. Every time I get involved in a major project, things go wrong."

Jumping to Conclusions

"That's just great. No media space means no launch. No launch means that the client will ditch us, and I'll be fired."

Blame

"I said at the beginning of this project that we'd have problems with the suppliers but I wasn't listened to. Now marketing has let us down just like I thought they would. How can I get things done when I'm always being let down."

Question

Ian's appraisal was generally very positive, but because a recent client briefing of his went badly, his boss suggested he work on his presentation skills.

Match the appropriate categories of negative thinking to Ian's thoughts.

Options:

A. focusing on the negative
B. all or nothing thinking
C. overgeneralization and labeling
D. jumping to conclusions
E. blame

Targets:

1. The projector was broken and the client hadn't read my report. What could I do?
2. The appraisal was a complete disaster. My boss has no confidence in me.
3. Every time I meet with a client or give a presentation, it goes wrong. I'm useless.
4. I won't be allowed to meet clients anymore, and so I won't ever get promoted.
5. I knew that the client briefing would let me down. I'm lucky everything else was OK.

Answer:

In fact, he labeled himself as useless, blamed the projector and his client, and jumped to conclusions about future promotions. He focused on the one negative part of his review, the briefing, and used all or nothing thinking in calling the review a disaster.

This is an example of blame. Ian is blaming the projector and the client for the problems with the presentation and not taking responsibility.

This is an example of all or nothing thinking. Ian is looking at things in black and white terms--he thinks he needs to improve his presentation skills and so everything is lost. He is also misreading his boss's comments.

This is an example of overgeneralization and labeling. Ian sees the problem with the client briefing as a single negative event and a never-ending pattern of defeat. He's also attached a negative label to himself.

This is an example of jumping to conclusions. Ian is "fortune-telling" by imagining that because of a single problem he'll be stopped from meeting clients and ultimately his career path will end. These are unrealistic negative outcomes.

This is an example of focusing on the negative. Ian is putting his boss's positive comments down to luck, and inflating the importance of his boss's comments about the briefing. He's allowing one bad comment to overshadow a good appraisal.

CATEGORIES OF NEGATIVE THINKING

Categories of negative thinking

So how can you overcome these negative thoughts?

You can apply four simple techniques to help you. You may find that you need to use all four techniques, or you might find that one of them works well for you.

The techniques are examining the evidence, befriending yourself, putting things in context, and looking for the positive.

Underpinning all of these techniques is a need to challenge your negative thinking.

Negative self-talk usually involves exaggeration of the negative, or imagining the worst. You need to look for the actual evidence of what happened rather than simply assuming that your version of the events is the correct one.

Examining the evidence relies on you knowing what happened and not relying on your perceptions--get feedback from trusted colleagues, review a report or schedule again, or go over feedback one more time. Examining the evidence is especially useful if you tend to jump to conclusions or engage in all or nothing thinking.

See each thinking process to find out more.

Jumping to Conclusions

Challenge your assumptions--why should everything go wrong? Are things as bad as you think?

All or Nothing

Not everything happens in black and white. Look at the elements of the event or problem--did some things go better than others, or did everything really go wrong?

Marcie, an events planner, often indulges in negative self-talk and is trying to challenge her thinking. Follow along to find out what her internal voice is saying.

You know, that sales conference was a complete disaster. Everyone was really unhappy with the food the hotel served, and no one enjoyed the main speaker.

Then again, when I asked Dana what she thought, she said the food was good. She also said that although the main speaker wasn't excellent, he made some good points.

I'm organizing another conference next month--I guess that'll be as bad as this one. We've hired a different speaker, but he'll probably be awful. And people are bound to complain about the food again.

Hold on. Why should the conference next month go badly? I've prepared for it, it's at a different hotel, and there's a different speaker. Do I have any reason to believe the food will be bad? When we've used this hotel before, it's always been excellent. I don't need to worry.

Marcie did a great job of challenging her negative thinking by examining the evidence. She started with all or nothing thinking, but then thought about what had really happened and challenged her perceptions by thinking about what Dana said.

Doing Business Professionally

When she found herself jumping to conclusions about the next conference, she checked herself by challenging those assumptions and looking for evidence to support them.

Question

You have a letter on your desk from a customer who has received a telemarketing call from your company. He says that he has asked to be removed from your call list several times, and now he's going to sue you and your company. You know that all requests for removal from the list have to be made in writing, and you wonder whether the customer has done this. You're worried that he could sue you and that this issue could affect your promotion.

Which of these statements use examining the evidence to overcome these negative thoughts?

Options:

1. I know he has to prove he's asked us to remove him from the list in writing. We don't have records of any letters.

2. That's it then. No need to worry about promotion--I won't have a job after I've been sued.

3. This is just one irate customer. I don't get hundreds of these letters each day. Why should it affect my promotion?

Answer:

Option 1: This option is correct. Examining the evidence involves looking at the facts and challenging your assumptions on that basis. In this case, the evidence suggests that the customer has no grounds to sue you, so you're worrying unnecessarily.

Option 2: This option is incorrect. The evidence in this situation is clear. There is no proof of the customer's claim, and if there were, there is no reason to believe you'll be fired. This is a clear example of negative thinking.

Option 3: This option is correct. Examining the evidence involves looking at the facts and challenging your assumptions. In this case, the evidence supports this as an isolated incident, and therefore it isn't likely to affect your future at the company.

Negative thinking turns you into your own worst enemy. Instead of beating yourself up, think about how you would react to a friend in a similar situation.

- What would you say?
- Would you be as harsh and judgmental as you're being to yourself?

Marcie's latest problem is a result of her ordering the wrong limousine to pick up her boss from the airport. Any of the techniques for challenging negative thinking will work in this situation, but befriending yourself is particularly effective.

Select each phase to find out Marcie's first thoughts and then what she did to befriend herself.

First thoughts

"I'm such a failure. Everything I do goes wrong. It was the wrong limousine today, and tomorrow I'll get the travel arrangements wrong--it'll just go downhill from there. I can't do anything right."

Befriending herself

"When Charlie messed up the limousine rental the other week, we didn't fire him or anything. We just reminded him which car the boss likes, and that was it.

Charlie wasn't fired, and there's no reason why my boss should fire me either."

Question

You recently dealt with a letter from a customer who was threatening to sue your company. You replied using a standard letter and explained that you had requested his removal from the list. He has now written to your boss to complain about the tone of your letter and your delay in replying. You feel that you can't do anything right and you're caught in a web of problems. Which of these choices use befriending yourself to overcome these negative thoughts?

Options:

1. I only did what anyone on the team would have done. I used the standard letter and replied as quickly as I could.

2. I'm sure that my colleagues wouldn't have made this type of mistake. It's all my fault. I'm useless.

3. If I were my boss, how would I react? I guess I might be frustrated, but that's all. It's just one of those things.

4. If I were my boss, I'd fire me on the spot.

Answer:

Option 1: This option is correct. Befriending yourself involves treating yourself in the same way you'd treat a friend or colleague. By looking at how another member of the team would be treated in the same situation, you can overcome your negative thoughts.

Option 2: This option is incorrect. Befriending yourself involves treating yourself in the same way you'd treat a friend or colleague. This doesn't mean engaging in more negative thoughts by comparing yourself unfavorably with colleagues.

Option 3: This option is correct. Befriending yourself involves treating yourself in the same way you'd treat a friend or colleague. By looking at how you'd react if you were in your boss's shoes, you can overcome your negative thoughts.

Option 4: This option is incorrect. Befriending yourself involves asking yourself, "Would I be as harsh and judgmental to a friend as I'm being to myself?" The answer to this question is usually no.

Putting things in context is a very straightforward technique to use, and it can help you dismiss some of your most extreme negative thoughts. It can also help you see the extent to which you're exaggerating the problems that you face. Asking yourself these questions will put your negative thoughts into context:

- Is what's happening a matter of life and death?
- What's the worst realistic outcome?
- How bad will it seem in a day, a week, or a month?
- Will I or anyone else remember this in time?

First the conference, then the limousine. Marcie's finding it hard to challenge her negative thinking. Follow along as she tries to put things in context.

I can't believe things are going so badly for me. I just can't get anything right. I can't begin to describe how nervous I am about the next conference.

It's possible nobody will like the food, the speaker won't show up, and I've booked the wrong cars for the VIPs. I'm a walking one-woman disaster.

All this worrying is making me sick--is it really that important? What's the worst that will happen if everything does go wrong? The delegates will complain and I'll have a warning from my boss. It's not a nice thought, but it's not life-threatening.

And next week, when it's all over and I'm organizing the next conference, what then? I probably won't even remember feeling like this, and I'm sure no one else will give a thought to my conference. I'm blowing things way out of proportion.

By putting things in context, Marcie realized she was overreacting to things that hadn't yet happened. She also recognized that even if everything went as badly as she imagined, the consequences weren't so bad--she'd feel embarrassed, uncomfortable, and maybe a little ashamed, but that's all.

As Marcie has shown, putting things in context is a very powerful technique that can help you overcome even the most extreme negative thoughts.

Question

It's midnight, and you can't keep your eyes open for a minute longer. You've been working on a status report for a client meeting the next day. Your choices are clear: go to sleep so that you are alert for the client meeting in the morning, or work to complete what will be a substandard report. You feel as if you're in a no-win situation, facing the possibility of losing the client and your job.

How can you put things in context to overcome these negative thoughts?

Options:

1. The client will either be frustrated that the report isn't finished or angry because I'm not at my best in the

meeting. The worst-case scenario is that I'll receive a warning from my boss.

2. I've dealt with problems like this in the past. It feels like the end of the world now, but it'll blow over in a few days.

3. This situation is making me ill. Stress can have long-term effects on health. This job is killing me.

4. If I don't finish this report, I'm finished. First I'll lose my job, and then I'll lose my home.

Answer:

Option 1: This option is correct. Putting things into context involves asking yourself what the worst realistic outcome of a situation is. In this case, it is frustration or anger on the client's behalf and possibly a warning from your boss. Neither of these is life-threatening.

Option 2: This option is correct. Putting things into context involves thinking about whether the current problem will still be an issue in the future. In this instance, past experience indicates the problem will likely blow over.

Option 3: This option is incorrect. Putting things into context involves thinking about realistic outcomes and considering whether a situation is truly life or death. Did anyone ever die because a report was late? This is negative thinking at its most extreme.

Option 4: This option is incorrect. Putting things into context involves challenging your negative thinking, not indulging further. This is an example of jumping to conclusions about how the client will react, how your boss will react, and what will happen to you.

The technique of looking for the positive is not only a way of overcoming negative thinking--it's a way of changing your outlook so that you look for the good in situations instead of the bad. In every situation, however bad, things could always be worse, and that's at the heart of looking for the positive.

Maybe the only good thing to draw from problems is that you'll learn from your mistakes, but often you can draw truly positive experiences from them.

If your slides didn't work in your presentation, you'll know to prepare more effectively next time. Was everything really a disaster? Maybe people commented favorably on your speaking voice, your choice of venue, and your knowledge of the product--all positive aspects of a "disastrous" presentation.

Marcie is at her wit's end. She's in the middle of a conference and there seem to be endless problems with the venue. The kitchen hasn't prepared the meals for delegates with special dietary requirements, there aren't enough seats in the conference auditorium, and the main speaker can't be heard at the back of the room. Marcie is determined not to be overcome by negative thoughts.

See each aspect of Marcie to find out how she looks for the positive.

Marcie 1

"I guess I should have checked with the kitchen to make sure they knew about the special meals. I'd sent a fax, but next time I'll know to speak to the restaurant manager and get confirmation. On the upside, most of the delegates are very pleased with their meals."

Marcie 2

"The feedback about our main speaker was excellent; I'll definitely use her again. It's just unfortunate that she couldn't be heard at the back because there was no microphone. In the future, I'll use a smaller room and limit the number of delegates."

Question

At a recent meeting, you failed to deliver a report. The client was frustrated that the report wasn't finished but agreed to listen to your conclusions. Unfortunately, the client wasn't pleased with your conclusions, and the meeting was brought to a sudden halt when he demanded to speak with your boss in private. After the client left, your boss explained that the client was embarrassed at some of your findings and felt you had behaved insensitively by presenting them in such unambiguous terms.

How can you use the techniques of looking for the positive in this situation?

Options:

1. The client was frustrated that my report wasn't complete, but he was still willing to hear my conclusions.

2. This just shows that the client is unreasonable. It's not my fault if he doesn't want to hear what I've got to say.

3. If I ever find myself in a situation like this again, I'll run through my conclusions with my boss first.

Answer:

Option 1: This option is correct. Looking for the positive involves finding something good in every situation. In this case, the client was still willing to listen to your conclusions even though the report wasn't complete.

Option 2: This option is incorrect. Looking for the positive involves finding something good in every situation. It doesn't involve finding ways to blame other people for your errors in judgment.

Option 3: This option is correct. Looking for the positive involves finding something good in every situation. In this case, things seemed very bad, but you can grow from the experience by improving how you present conclusions to clients.

When you challenge your negative thinking, you'll learn valuable lessons from the situations you face, and you'll be able to avoid overreacting to or overdramatizing problems that can be solved.

Whatever technique you use to challenge negative thinking, your focus must be on being realistic and objective in your responses to situations. Each of the four techniques has at its core a recognition that things are rarely as bad as you perceive them to be.

Don't challenge everything your inner voice tells you. Only challenge those things that are having a destructive influence on your state of mind.

If the voice in your head says "You shouldn't have been late," this is a rational and useful comment, not a harmful negative thought.

It isn't always possible to ignore the voice in your head that criticizes you and undermines your confidence.

But that doesn't mean you have to believe what the voice says.

Challenge the voice, and challenge your negative thoughts. You'll find that positive thinking can help you find the best in the situations you face.

REACT POSITIVELY TO CRITICISM OR FEEDBACK

React positively to criticism or feedback

Unfortunately, you don't have control over what people say to you--but you do have control over how you respond.

One of the most difficult times to respond to someone is when you are being criticized, particularly when that criticism does not appear to be constructive or even justified.

An inability to accept or handle criticism, even when it's constructive and in your best interest, results in a negative attitude toward both the criticism itself and the critic.

The key to reacting positively to criticism is to take three simple actions:
- agree with the truth of the criticism,
- agree with the logic of the critic,
- acknowledge that improvement is possible.

If there is truth in the criticism, acknowledge this when dealing with the critic, and don't avoid the issue. When criticism is aimed at something you're uncomfortable talking about, you often dispute even undeniable facts to try to halt the conversation, but this usually has the opposite effect.

See the advice to find out more about how to accept the truth.

Do

Do agree with the truth, and if appropriate, apologize. Saying that the critic is right and that you're sorry is a good way of putting an end to the conversation.

Don't

Don't deny the facts of the situation, even if you feel you've been unfairly treated. Making excuses, arguing about whose fault it is, or trying to shift blame away from yourself will only extend the criticism.

Oliver and Jim are working together on a building project. Oliver has asked to speak to Jim about the fact that the project is behind schedule. Follow along to find out how Jim reacts.

Oliver: I'm concerned that you haven't hit the deadline on the phase 1 deliverables you agreed to.

Jim: That's not true. I've done everything I said I would.

Oliver: Well, you put the schedule together, and you don't seem to know what you're supposed to be doing. You haven't finished the interim report, which was due yesterday.

Jim's negative approach to Oliver's criticism resulted in an escalation of the problem--and more stress for Jim.

Instead of admitting that he'd missed the deadline, Jim became defensive and denied the truth, which simply resulted in Oliver criticizing him further for failing to review the schedule properly.

Now follow along to find out what happens when Jim agrees with the truth of Oliver's criticism.

Oliver: I'm concerned that you haven't hit the deadline on the phase 1 deliverables you agreed to.

Jim: I know I haven't finished the interim report. I'm sorry. I took on too much and now I'm finding it difficult to meet my commitments.

This time, Jim wasn't negative. He admitted that he'd missed the deadline and immediately defused the situation with Oliver.

Question

You're a research assistant for a paint manufacturing company. You've been asked to create variations on white paints, but you've found it difficult to generate new ideas because there are so many variations already available. At your team meeting, your colleagues are asked to comment on your work. One of your colleagues comments negatively by saying, "You haven't come up with anything new." What are some of the responses you could use to agree with the truth of the critic's comments?

Options:

1. Well, I have found it difficult to generate new ideas.

2. That's true. A lot of the work on white has already been done.

3. That's not true. I've come up with some really innovative new ideas.

4. Because we've done so much work on white in the past, there's nothing left to create.

Answer:

Option 1: This option is correct. Agreeing with the truth of the critic's comments, however negative, is a good way of defusing a difficult situation. Although the critic has been harsh, it is true to say that you've found it difficult to generate new ideas.

Option 2: This option is correct. Agreeing with the truth of the critic's comments means admitting that you didn't generate new ideas. This response does agree with the critic in a nonconfrontational way.

Option 3: This option is incorrect. Agreeing with the truth of the critic's comments means just that. You found it difficult to generate new ideas, and you should admit it. Denying the fact will lead to confrontation when the critic asks you to justify your response.

Option 4: This option is incorrect. To agree with the truth of the critic's comments, you should admit that you found it difficult to generate new ideas. Making excuses for your performance won't deflect criticism--it will increase it.

A critic's perspective on a situation will be different from yours. As a result, you might feel that a critic is being unfair. You must accept that the critic has a valid view and that his suggestion might work, even if you don't adhere to his thinking.

Agreeing with the logic doesn't mean saying you'll take action.

If your critic proposes a solution that you're reluctant to adopt, simply agree that his suggestion is a good one without committing to take action.

Don't argue with acceptable and reasonable logic, and don't attack the critic--this will lead to an argument.

Follow along as Jim agrees with the logic of Oliver's suggestion.

Oliver: How about we work on it together to see if we can finish the interim report now? I've got time if you have.

Jim: That's not a bad idea, but I've got a lot of information at my desk. Can I review it and get back to you?

Oliver: Well, let me know how you want to proceed. I'm anxious to get back on track.

When Oliver suggested that they work together on the interim report, Jim agreed that Oliver's suggestion was a good one; in other words, he accepted the logic of what Oliver said. However, even though he accepted Oliver's logic, he did not accept the offer of help.

That way, Jim knew that Oliver would feel like Jim was open to his suggestion but Jim didn't have to commit to doing things Oliver's way. Both parties were pleased with the outcome.

Question

One of your colleagues is criticizing the work you've done on a line of white paint. She has already been negative about your ideas, and now she suggests that you review your company's archive for inspiration. She also puts forward some ideas for themes that you might consider. You've already looked at the company archive, and you find her tone patronizing.

What could you say to agree with the logic of the critic's comments?

Options:

1. The themes you've suggested are very obvious. I would have thought that with your apparent expertise, you'd have suggested something more innovative.

2. Reviewing the archive is a good strategy--there's some interesting material there.

3. There is merit in the idea of using themes--whatever they might be.

4. I've already looked at the archive. It's an obvious place to start.

Answer:

Option 1: This option is incorrect. Although your colleague is being patronizing, there is logic in her argument and you should concede. This sarcastic and combative response will only make things worse. Turning on the critic is not constructive.

Option 2: This option is correct. Agreeing with the logic of the critic's comments means admitting that the critic's view is valid. This response agrees that using the archive is a good idea and hints at the fact that you've used it, without being combative.

Option 3: This option is correct. Agreeing with the logic of the critic's comments doesn't mean agreeing to take action. This response acknowledges that the use of themes is valid, but avoids committing to investigating the themes suggested.

Option 4: This option is incorrect. The fact that you have already looked at the archive shows that your critic is making a logical suggestion, even if you feel that she is being patronizing. You should simply agree with her and resist the temptation to attack.

However much you might feel that there's nothing more that can be done, you need to step back and think rationally about what the critic is saying.

It may well be that you can change things to improve the situation--unless things are perfect already.

When your critic suggests that you could do better, respond by saying, "There may be some areas that could improve." This is a good way of acknowledging that improvement is possible while avoiding committing to changes.

It's tempting to claim that you can't do any better, or even to attack the critic's own abilities, but this only escalates bad feelings. If you reverse the criticism by challenging the critic, he'll try to prove you wrong--and the disagreement will escalate.

Follow along to find out what happens when Jim challenges Oliver's criticism instead of accepting that there may be room for improvement.

Oliver: Have you decided how to proceed? As I said, I'm more than willing to help you create the report if it will help us get back on track. After all, something has to be done.

Jim: I don't need your help, Oliver. I said I'll do it, and I will. I'm doing the best I can.

Oliver: Well, that's easy to say, but we're already behind. We need to find a way of getting back on track, and staying there.

Jim: So, you think you can do better, do you? Fine. Here's my information. You can write the report.

Oliver: At least if I do it myself, I'll know it's going to get done. I was only trying to help. There was no need for you to react so aggressively.

Jim clearly felt threatened by Oliver's criticism and didn't want to accept that there was anything he could do to improve the situation. Instead of graciously declining Oliver's offer of help, Jim became hostile toward Oliver and turned the criticism back on him.

As a result, Oliver criticized Jim for being aggressive. Needless to say, Jim and Oliver's relationship deteriorated.

Now follow along to find out how different things are when Jim acknowledges that improvement is possible.

Oliver: Have you decided how to proceed? As I said, I'm more than willing to help you create the report if it will help us get back on track. After all, something has to be done.

Jim: I agree. I've taken on too much. That's why I'm behind schedule.

Oliver: So, what's the solution?

Jim: I'll focus on getting the report finished, and then I'll review the schedule. If we can get together later in the day, we can look at the schedule together.

This time, Jim wasn't combative. Although he didn't want help from Oliver, Jim reacted calmly and reasonably to Oliver's request for an update. By admitting that he had taken on too much work, he was acknowledging that there was room for improvement.

Jim could have stopped there, but he went a step further and committed to reviewing the schedule to avoid future problems. Hopefully, this additional step will keep Oliver from voicing future criticism.

Question

As your team meeting draws to a close, the team leader begins to summarize the discussion and allocate action points. One of your colleagues can't resist an opportunity to make another unhelpful comment about the work you've done on a line of white paints. She says "Don't forget that the line of variations you created needs to be completely reworked--this time with some imagination."

What are some ways to acknowledge that improvement is possible?

Options:

1. I certainly haven't exhausted all of the possibilities yet.
2. Why don't I just remove myself from this project altogether? You can present your ideas at the next meeting.
3. That's very unfair. I've done my best to come up with ideas. I can't do any more.
4. I was thinking about revisiting some of my initial ideas and possibly canvassing for ideas. There must be something I've missed.

Answer:

Option 1: This option is correct. It is possible for you to generate more ideas, and this is a good way to acknowledge that you could improve what you've done. It also doesn't commit you to a course of action at this point.

Option 2: This option is incorrect. Rarely can you say that what you've done is perfect--there is always room to improve. Reversing the criticism onto your colleague may give you some satisfaction, but it makes you seem petty and encourages further conflict.

Option 3: This option is incorrect. There is always room to improve, even if you feel that you've given everything. This response will simply lead to further criticism from your colleague, who can now accuse you of feeling sorry for yourself.

Option 4: This option is correct. You're acknowledging that you could improve the line you've created without being explicit about what you'll do.

Agreeing with the truth and logic of criticism isn't a commitment to behavioral change. Neither is acknowledging that improvement is possible. These three approaches merely limit the potential conflict that could arise from your instinctive need to retaliate.

They help you to avoid feeling bad about yourself, even when the criticism is justified. By agreeing with the critic verbally, you'll avoid negative feelings and be able to react positively to the feedback or criticism that you receive.

Remember, you have control over how you react to other's comments. Use that control to your advantage, and let it help you to develop a positive attitude and react positively to the feedback that you receive.

OVERCOMING NEGATIVE IMPACT

Overcoming negative impact

Feeling out of control is one of the most common triggers for negative thinking. If you feel as if you can't influence what happens to you, then you begin to lack confidence and believe the worst is inevitable.

One of the best ways to cope with situations that make you feel negative is to define your boundaries-- that means defining what you will or will not tolerate. To do this, you need to be assertive. There are two steps you need to follow:

- Get attention.
- Command a positive response.

When you're asked to do something you don't want to do, it can be tempting to be aggressive or defensive, or to simply concede without discussion.

Being assertive means stating your case in a forceful manner, without being aggressive.

If you feel like you're being taken advantage of, or if you simply don't want to comply with a request, you need to get the attention of the person doing the requesting.

Getting attention doesn't mean being rude or unhelpful--that gets you noticed for all of the wrong reasons. It means finding a time when it's appropriate to talk and then calmly explaining your perspective.

See the advice to find out about the two aspects of getting attention.

Choosing the time

You should deal with issues quickly, but you want to choose a time when you aren't feeling angry or irritated. It's often a good idea to wait until after you've had a "cooling off" period. You should also make sure you can discuss the issue without distractions.

Explaining the facts

You need to explain why you are unhappy or unwilling to comply with a request. Avoid language that is critical or accusatory, and stick to the facts of the situation. It is also helpful to offer a concession to the other person to show that you are being reasonable.

Ted and Michelle work together. Michelle isn't good at organizing her time, and when deadlines approach, she often relies on Ted to help her out. Follow along as Michelle asks Ted for help yet again.

Michelle: Ted, I know you're busy, but I'm in a fix. I haven't finished the programming for the phase 1 prototype, and it has to be finished by Tuesday. You don't mind working the weekend with me to get it finished do you?

Ted: Can we talk about this later Michelle? I'm in the middle of an important piece of work at the moment.

Michelle: Oh, OK. I guess so. Later then.

Ted has been feeling negative about the way his colleagues take advantage of him, and so he is trying a new tactic--being assertive.

See each person to find out more about Ted and Michelle's reactions to their recent exchange.

Ted

"Michelle always does this, and it isn't fair. I have my own work to do. I was so angry with her today that I had to take some time to calm down"

Michelle

"I can't believe it. Usually Ted is such a soft touch. He's a nice guy and will always help out. We all know that we can rely on 'good old Ted.'"

Ted has decided that he isn't prepared to help Michelle this weekend because he has personal and work commitments of his own. Follow along as Ted catches up with Michelle during a coffee break.

Ted: Michelle, have you got time to talk?

Michelle: Sure, I'm on a break. I guess you want to talk about what you can

do to help me with this programming. I don't think it will take all weekend.

Ted: The thing is, Michelle, I have commitments of my own this weekend. I'm behind on one of my own projects, so I need to work on that, and I've also promised to take my son to his Little League game.

Michelle: Oh.

Ted: I know you were hoping I could help out, but I don't have a lot of time. I could try to free up some time tomorrow morning or on Monday if that helps.

Ted did a great job of getting Michelle's attention. He didn't talk to her when he was feeling angry; he waited until he had time to think about her request and calm down.

When he did speak to Michelle, he chose a time when they could speak openly and without distractions. Although Michelle assumed that Ted was going to agree to her request fully, Ted stuck to his strategy and explained the facts.

By telling Michelle why he was unable to help her out, he was reasonable and fair. He also offered a concession by offering time, during working hours, to support her.

Question

Your organization has a state-of-the-art research facility, and visitors are often invited to look around. Responsibility for visitors should be shared between the members of your team, but this week you've dealt with four groups of visitors--and your colleague Helen hasn't dealt with any. You're frustrated that she has managed to avoid doing this, and you decide to speak to her.

What will you do to get her attention?

Options:

1. Send her an e-mail and schedule an appointment to talk to her.

2. Find her immediately and tell her how upset you are about having to deal with so many visitors.

3. Remind her that responsibility for visitors should be shared, and that although you're always willing to step in for an emergency, you don't have time to deal with all of the visitors.

4. Remind her that responsibility for visitors should be shared, and that she hasn't been pulling her weight.

Answer:

Option 1: This option is correct. The first aspect of getting Helen's attention is to make sure that you speak to her when you are calm, and when there are no distractions. Scheduling an appointment is a good way to do this.

Option 2: This option is incorrect. The first aspect of getting Helen's attention is to make sure that you speak to her when you are calm--in this case that means giving yourself a little time to cool off. You also need to find a time when there are no distractions. Scheduling an appointment is a good way to do this.

Option 3: This option is correct. The second aspect of getting Helen's attention is to explain the facts of the situation, without being confrontational. In this case, you also offer a concession by agreeing that you are prepared to step in for emergencies.

Option 4: This option is incorrect. The second aspect of getting Helen's attention is to explain the facts of the situation, without being confrontational. By suggesting that Helen is neglecting her responsibilities you are being accusatory and aggressive.

Once you have the attention of the person you're trying to negotiate with, you need to get the response you want-- a positive one. It isn't always easy to get the response you're looking for. Being assertive means working on your own behalf to secure an outcome that you're happy with.

See the advice to find out more about the main aspects of commanding a positive response.

asking for help

When you've made the other person aware of the facts of your situation, you need to get him to buy-in to helping you. You can do this by inviting him to change the situation or by getting him to see the problem from your perspective. Remain calm and reasonable, even if the response is negative.

recycling your message

Show that you would appreciate a serious offer, possibly to withdraw the request or to compromise. If no offer is forthcoming or if you disagree with the other person's proposal, make a proposal yourself. Being assertive means being forceful and not caving in to pressure at this point.

Ted and Michelle's discussion moves on as Ted tries to command a positive response from Michelle. Follow along to find out what happens.

Michelle: You're telling me you don't have the time to help me? I don't believe this. I rely on you to pitch in and help at the last minute. I don't know what I'm going to do. How can you let me down like this?

Ted: To be fair, Michelle, I think you need to look at this from where I'm standing. I've got my own work to do, and my own commitments.

Michelle: Whatever. So you're saying you can help me tomorrow and on Monday, right?

Ted: That's right. I can help you tomorrow morning or on Monday. I can't do more than that.

Michelle: I'd appreciate your help tomorrow morning if that's OK with you. I'll work the weekend and see what happens on Monday. Thanks, Ted.

Ted did a great job of commanding a positive response. Despite Michelle's initial disbelief, Ted continued to be assertive by getting her to look at things from his perspective.

When Michelle came back to Ted with a proposal--to use the time that Ted had offered--he recycled his message by restating the facts without giving in to Michelle.

At the end of the discussion, Ted had a positive response from Michelle. Instead of agreeing to all of her demands, he responded assertively to Michelle and reached a compromise that both he and Michelle were happy with.

A positive outcome for both sides.

Being assertive can help you halt negative feelings.

Question

You explain to your colleague, Helen, that she should share responsibility for showing visitors around your organization's research facility. Unfortunately, Helen simply shrugs her shoulders and tells you she's too busy to get involved, and that she doesn't understand why you can't continue filling in.

What will you do to command a positive response from Helen?

Options:

1. Tell her that you're already doing more than your share, and that you're not doing it anymore.

2. Tell her that you're doing more than your share, and suggest that you create a list of visitors and allocate them fairly.

3. Explain to Helen that you're busy too, and that having to always deal with all of the visitors is affecting your ability to do a good job.

4. Explain to Helen that she can't get away with such a dismissive attitude--two can play at that game.

Answer:

Option 1: This option is incorrect. The second aspect of commanding a positive response involves recycling your

Doing Business Professionally

message to secure a serious offer from Helen. This response doesn't help anyone because you're failing to compromise.

Option 2: This option is correct. The second aspect of commanding a positive response involves recycling your message to secure a serious offer from Helen. In this case, no offer is forthcoming, and so making your own proposal is the best way forward.

Option 3: This option is correct. The first aspect of commanding a positive response involves getting Helen to see things from your perspective. Explaining your situation to Helen and highlighting how her actions affect you is a good way to do this.

Option 4: This option is incorrect. The first aspect of commanding a positive response involves getting Helen to see things from your perspective. It's important to do this by remaining calm--you don't want to get involved in petty arguments.

To reach a position where you and Adam can share a desk amicably, you need to be assertive. Choosing a time when you can approach the issue in a calm and rational way is the first step to getting Adam's attention and to reaching a resolution.

When you do talk to Adam about the desk, it's important to explain the issue in a factual way with no hint of personal criticism or accusation.

Sometimes, no matter how much you hint at a solution, it is necessary to put forward your own proposal to command a positive response.

This should always be done in a nonaccusatory, and nonjudgmental way if you are to get the outcome you seek.

Sorin Dumitrascu

You are entitled to insist on having your boundaries respected, and assertiveness steps are powerful tools to enable you to do this. Identify situations where it is appropriate and start to use them.

PURSUING SUCCESSFUL LIFELONG LEARNING

Pursuing Successful Lifelong Learning

So you want to climb the corporate ladder, do you? Or maybe you've been thinking about changing careers. Perhaps you've never had a job, or it has been years since you had one.

No matter your circumstances or dreams for the future, one thing is certain: you're going to have to learn new skills and behaviors if you want to move from where you are in life to where you want to be.

"You've got to be very careful if you don't know where you are going because you might not get there." - -Yogi Berra, baseball player and coach

Yogi Berra was gifted at stating the obvious, often with hilarious results. But his comments were also grounded in common sense.

Of course you won't get where you're going if you don't know where you're going. But it's amazing how many people assume that they will achieve their dreams even though they haven't developed a strategy to do so.

How would you define the word "objective"? A goal is the end to which you direct your efforts.

Objectives are often used to help people reach their goals. For the lifelong learner, an objective is often known as a learning objective. Learning objectives are statements that explain exactly what the learner will be able to do at the conclusion of instructional activities.

Lifelong learners apply learning objectives to their learning plan after they have identified the specific skills, knowledge, and abilities they want to acquire or enhance.

Imagine you've identified your learning needs, determined your learning goals, and constructed the appropriate learning objectives. All you need to do now is achieve those objectives, right?

In fact, you need to develop a learning strategy and a way to evaluate the learning objectives you've set. The last two sections of your learning plan will allow you to do just that.

How will you go about attaining new skills or improving existing ones to achieve your professional dreams?

Successful lifelong learners know that after developing their learning objectives, they should develop a learning strategy for each objective.

No learning strategy is complete if it doesn't include a way for you to verify whether you have accomplished each task.

In many learning plans, this information is contained in the fourth section: means for evaluation. A learning plan is a written road map for initiating and continuing career and professional development.

Take a minute to think back over your life. Does anyone stand out as being particularly helpful or insightful? Did anyone ever challenge you--in a way that bolstered your self-esteem--to work harder and become more proficient at something?

Some people remember one or two teachers, coaches, troop leaders, religious leaders, or college advisors who made a difference in their lives.

Imagine that you and several others have been shipwrecked on an island. Only one person in your group can speak the same language as the locals.

Like the island spokesperson, a mentor is a compassionate person who influences your fate. A mentor is someone with a great deal of experience and influence in a chosen field who helps and guides your-- the protege's--professional or career development.

Have you ever been in a relationship where you feel as though the other person is always calling the shots? If so, how did that make you feel? Did you ever do anything that you wanted to do?

Mentoring offers you the opportunity to accept guidance and input from an expert in your field; it should not entail handing over complete control of your professional life.

LEARNING NEEDS AND LEARNING OBJECTIVES

Learning needs and learning objectives

So you want to climb the corporate ladder, do you? Or maybe you've been thinking about changing careers. Perhaps you've never had a job, or it has been years since you had one.

No matter your circumstances or dreams for the future, one thing is certain: you're going to have to learn new skills and behaviors if you want to move from where you are in life to where you want to be.

But before you jump into learning those new skills and behaviors, it's a good idea to first determine what it is you want, what it is you need, and what it is you have to do to get what you want and need.

Making these determinations will help you identify your learning needs and establish your learning objectives.

Learning needs are the skills and knowledge that must be acquired for career and professional development to occur.

Doing Business Professionally

Learning objectives are statements that explain what you will be able to do at the conclusion of instructional activities.

It's important that you identify your learning needs because this process will enhance your self-awareness and make it easier to establish the right learning objectives for you.

Establishing the right learning objectives is important because they will keep you on the path toward your goals.

Take Carrie, for example. After she earned her bachelor's degree in liberal arts, Carrie was offered a job as copywriter in an advertising agency. She had always been creative, so she accepted the position.

But after two years of creative copywriting while on tight deadlines, Carrie was exhausted and dissatisfied; she didn't know what she wanted to do, but she knew that copywriting wasn't it. Right around that time, she met Ben, a career counselor whom she started to work with.

Follow along as Carrie explains how Ben helped her understand the importance of identifying her learning needs.

"The first thing Ben had me do was identify my learning needs. I did this by writing down my values, my interests, and the skills I like to use. Until I did this exercise, I thought I knew who I was. But I had never really taken the time to sit down and think about it."

"It turns out that even though I'm creative, being able to be creative at work isn't something I am all that interested in. And even though I like writing, it isn't a skill that I want to use all the time."

"Instead, I like to feel that I'm making a difference; I like children and would be very interested in working more with them. And I'd like to use the knowledge I gained about history and my interest in current events on a much more regular basis."

"If I hadn't sat down and really evaluated what was important to me, I wouldn't have known these things about myself. Also, I would have created learning objectives that had nothing to do with how I truly feel. I might have wound up in yet another job I didn't like."

By identifying her learning needs, Carrie became more self-aware. That self-awareness made it easier for her to establish the right learning objectives.

See each action to learn how Carrie established learning objectives.

Identifying learning needs

"After identifying my learning needs, I realized that what I really wanted to do was teach history and civics."

Developing learning objectives

"Ben asked me a lot of questions about my decision to become a teacher. My answers became the learning objectives that would help me reach my goal."

Carrie knew she wanted to be a teacher, but didn't know what grade level she wanted to teach. So one of her first objectives was to identify which grade level appealed to her the most. She also didn't have a teaching certificate; obviously, she was going to need to get one, and that became another objective.

All of Carrie's learning objectives specifically pointed her in the direction she needed to go to reach her goal of becoming a teacher. By planning in advance as Ben suggested, Carrie knew what she wanted to do and how to get there.

Question

When taking charge of your own learning, it's important that you first identify your learning needs and establish your learning objectives. Select the reasons why.

Options:

1. You'll learn more about yourself.

2. You'll be able to establish the right learning objectives for you.

3. You'll know which direction you need to go in to reach your goals.

4. You'll be able to enhance your ability to communicate effectively.

5. You'll get the knowledge you need to succeed.

6. You'll be able to increase your coping abilities.

Answer:

Option 1: This choice is correct. Identifying your learning needs will help you learn more about yourself. What you learn about yourself through this process may very well surprise you.

Option 2: This choice is correct. Identifying your learning needs will help you establish the right learning objectives for you. That's because you will have identified what you value, what interests you, and what skills you want to use regularly.

Option 3: Correct. Establishing your learning objectives will provide you with your direction in reaching your goals. Because you will have prepared these objectives in advance, you will know exactly what you need to do each step along the way.

Option 4: Incorrect. Identifying your learning needs and establishing your learning objectives may help you determine what you need to learn to communicate effectively, but you still have to do the work.

Option 5: This choice is incorrect. Identifying your learning needs and establishing your learning objectives will not provide you with the knowledge you need to succeed unless you take action on your identified needs.

Option 6: This choice is incorrect. Once you identify your learning needs and establish your learning objectives, you may realize that you need to increase your coping skills, but you must then seek that information and incorporate it if you actually want to improve.

The first step toward becoming a lifelong learner is to develop a learning plan. A learning plan is a written road map for initiating and continuing your career and professional development. This lesson covers the first two sections of a learning plan: career assessment and career focus.

Career assessment offers you the chance to examine your career values, interests, and motivating skills. You will use this information to identify your learning needs.

Career focus centers around your goals, the learning objectives that will help you achieve those goals, and the tasks you will have to undertake to accomplish your objectives.

THE CAREER ASSESSMENT SECTION OF A LEARNING PLAN

The career assessment section of a learning plan
"You've got to be very careful if you don't know where you are going because you might not get there." - -Yogi Berra, baseball player and coach

Yogi Berra was gifted at stating the obvious, often with hilarious results. But his comments were also grounded in common sense.

Of course you won't get where you're going if you don't know where you're going. But it's amazing how many people assume that they will achieve their dreams even though they haven't developed a strategy to do so.

The first step toward knowing where you're going--in other words, toward creating a learning plan--is to identify your learning needs. Learning needs are the skills and knowledge that must be acquired for career and professional development to occur.

To identify your learning needs, you can take career assessments and engage in self-discovery activities. Career assessments are made up of questions designed to help you identify your skills and career interests.

Self-discovery activities are assessments you can take and games you can play to learn more about yourself. Many people engage in self-discovery activities that help pinpoint their values and personality traits.

The first section of your learning plan, career assessment, should pertain to your identified learning needs. Specifically, this section should contain information about:

- your career values,
- your career interests,
- the job skills that motivate you.

Career values are concepts and views that define your professional beliefs and principles. Examples of career values include life-work balance, order and structure, glamour, independence, teamwork, and customer focus.

See each factor to learn how various people act at work to demonstrate their career values.

life-work balance

Seth is a financial analyst who values life-work balance. He is married with three children, and he is a competitive cyclist. He works efficiently to meet client expectations in an average of eight hours a day so that he can attend to his other priorities at the end of his workday.

order and structure

Denise is an accounts payable manager who values order and structure. Her profession allows her to follow a predictable schedule and explicitly stated rules. She has a routine for processing, accounting, and financial reporting of accounts payable transactions.

glamour

Devin enjoys an alluring lifestyle as an international management consultant. He is responsible for high-profile accounts. He travels to Paris, London, Amsterdam, Tokyo, and Hong Kong to analyze and propose ways to improve organizational structure, efficiency, and profits.

independence

Nancy is a journalist who values independence. She likes to determine the nature of her work without significant direction from others. She selects the focus and content of her newspaper articles with limited input from others.

teamwork

Michelle is part of a web design team that works closely to create winning web solutions. The team collaborates to assess customer needs, create web designs, and address customer issues. It uses collaborative software to share files, data, and projects.

customer focus

Harry is a technical support engineer who values customer focus. He places the interests of clients ahead of personal or organizational interests. Harry seeks feedback from clients and incorporates the feedback to improve quality, productivity, and customer service.

Paul is a senior technical support engineer who is responsible for providing quality technical support to internal and external customers. This involves supporting, analyzing, and testing his company's software.

Paul provides team members with assistance in resolving customer issues and completing support projects. He enjoys the challenge of applying his knowledge to problems presented by customers.

Paul feels job satisfaction when customers and colleagues express their gratitude for his assistance.

Which career values pertain to Paul?

The career values that pertain to Paul are appreciation, problem solving, and mental challenge.

See each value, in order, to learn more about how it applies to Paul.

Appreciation

Paul values being acknowledged in private for his efforts. When customers express their gratitude for his assistance, he feels a sense of job satisfaction.

Problem Solving

Paul values problem solving, or working to remove obstacles and finding solutions to difficult problems. He helps customers find solutions to their problems.

Mental Challenges

Paul values the mental challenge presented by his work. He is involved in activities that allow him to exercise his knowledge of his company's software.

The career assessment section also includes career interests. Career interests are professional fields that are best suited for you based on your preferences. These interests can be placed into six categories: hands-on, scientific, artistic, social, enterprising, and conventional.

See each category of career interests to learn more.

hands-on

People who prefer to work with animals, tools, or machines are interested in hands-on careers. They are skilled with tools, mechanical or electrical drawings, machines, plants, or animals.

scientific

People who prefer solving math and science problems are interested in scientific careers. They typically avoid leading, selling, or persuading activities. Those interested in scientific careers see themselves as precise, methodical, and intellectual.

artistic

People who gravitate toward creative activities such as visual art, dance, music, or writing are interested in artistic careers. They generally avoid highly ordered or repetitive activities. They see themselves as expressive, original, and independent.

social

People who like to engage in activities that help people, such as teaching, nursing, giving first aid, or informing, have an interest in social careers. They avoid using machines or tools to achieve goals. They see themselves as helpful, friendly, and trustworthy.

enterprising

People who enjoy leading and persuading others, as well as selling products and ideas, have an interest in enterprising careers. They avoid activities that require careful observation and analytical thinking. They perceive themselves as energetic, ambitious, and sociable.

conventional

People who prefer to work with numbers, records, or machines in an orderly way are interested in conventional careers. They avoid ambiguous, unstructured activities. They perceive themselves as orderly and good at following a set plan.

After you have determined your career interests, the next step is to identify the occupations that fall within your category of interest.

See each career interest category to find examples of occupations associated with it.

Hands-on

Examples of hands-on occupations include mechanical engineer, ultrasound technologist, carpenter, microelectronics technician, firefighter, and geologist.

Scientific

Examples of scientific occupations include surgeon, botanist, anthropologist, psychiatrist, software engineer, and market research analyst.

Artistic

Examples of artistic occupations include architect, screenwriter, fashion designer, choreographer, sculptor, photojournalist, music teacher, and cartoonist.

Social

Examples of social occupations include nurse-midwife, coach, teacher, social worker, employee relations specialist, minister, loan officer, and physical therapist.

Enterprising

Examples of enterprising occupations include communications consultant, patent agent, art director, tax attorney, motion pictures producer, industrial-health engineer, and advertising sales representative.

Conventional

Examples of conventional occupations include credit analyst, medical record technician, accountant, and computer operator.

Most people will feel an affinity toward several of the six categories of career interests. And many of the combinations are complementary.

For example, if you prefer to work with animals and you enjoy science and math, your interests lie within the hands-on and scientific categories. These two categories can be combined to provide a variety of occupations that may appeal to you, such as veterinarian, marine biologist, or wildlife conservationist.

Learning about your career interests can also help you identify occupations that probably won't fulfill your needs.

For example, if your interests lie within the social and artistic categories, becoming a surgeon is probably not an ideal occupation for you.

Remember Paul, the senior technical support engineer responsible for providing quality technical support to internal and external customers? He assists team members in resolving customer issues and completing support projects and enjoys the challenge of solving technical problems encountered by customers.

Think about what his top two categories of career interests and his preferred occupations might be. See each of Paul's preferences to verify your conclusions.

Paul's career interests

Paul's top two categories of career interests are scientific and social. He enjoys solving problems related to his company's software, and he gets satisfaction from helping his customers.

Paul's preferred occupations

Paul's preferred occupations are software trainer and computer support specialist. Trainers instruct learners in the use of software applications. Support specialists interpret problems and provide technical support for hardware, software, and systems.

Case Study: Question 1 of 3
Scenario

Sean, a layout artist with a publishing company, is responsible for laying out images and text in an attractive format. He has enjoyed his work but is ready for a change.

Select career values and interests to learn about the career values and interests that apply to Sean. Then answer the questions that follow, in order.

Career Values

"I enjoy creating visually pleasing graphics for business applications. I like

working with people occasionally, but prefer autonomous work that calls for self- expression through images. I prefer not to collaborate with others or supervise others."

Career Interests

"I enjoy creative pursuits such as illustrating and painting. I see myself as expressive, original, and independent. I enjoy working with tangible tools, such as computer software and hardware. I don't enjoy performing structured, orderly, planned tasks."

Question

What are Sean's career values?

Options:

1. cooperation
2. independence
3. artistic creativity
4. innovation
5. glamour

Answer:

Option 1: This choice is not correct. Sean prefers not to collaborate with or supervise others. He would rather work autonomously.

Option 2: This option is correct. One of Sean's career values is independence. He enjoys being able to determine the nature of his work without significant input from others.

Option 3: This choice is correct. Artistic creativity is one of Sean's career values. He enjoys creating visually pleasing graphics for business applications.

Option 4: This option is incorrect. There is no indication that Sean enjoys working on the frontiers of knowledge. Rather, he gets satisfaction from creative expression.

Option 5: This option is incorrect. There is no indication that Sean is drawn to an alluring and glamorous lifestyle.

Case Study: Question 2 of 3

What are Sean's top two career interests?

Options:

1. social
2. artistic
3. scientific
4. hands-on
5. conventional

Answer:

Option 1: This choice is not correct. One of Sean's career interests is not social; he likes autonomous work that calls for self-expression through images. He prefers not to collaborate with or supervise others.

Option 2: This choice is correct. Sean's preferred career interest is artistic. He sees himself as expressive, original, and independent, and he dislikes repetitive or ordered activities that require minimal creativity.

Option 3: This option is not correct. Sean is not interested in solving math and science problems. He doesn't see himself as precise, scientific, and intellectual. Rather, he sees himself as expressive, original, and independent.

Option 4: This choice is correct. One of Sean's top two career interests is hands-on. He enjoys working with tangible tools, such as computer software and hardware.

Option 5: This choice is incorrect. Sean is not interested in conventional careers. He dislikes performing structured, orderly, planned tasks. Instead, he enjoys work that allows for creative expression and originality.

Case Study: Question 3 of 3

Given Sean's preferred career interests, which occupations do you think he would be interested in pursuing?

Options:

1. art director
2. media software trainer
3. graphic designer
4. architectural drafter
5. illustrator
6. multimedia designer

Answer:

Option 1: This option is incorrect. An art director is an enterprising occupation because it involves leading and persuading others. Sean's preferred career interests are artistic and hands-on, not enterprising.

Option 2: This choice is incorrect. A media software trainer is classified as a social occupation. This occupation involves helping and informing others as they cultivate their artistic skills. Sean's preferred career interests are artistic and hands-on, not social.

Option 3: This option is correct. A graphic designer is classified as an artistic occupation because it involves conceptualizing and creating graphically pleasing designs. This is one of Sean's preferred career interests.

Option 4: This is correct. An architectural drafter is classified as a hands-on occupation; it involves operating computer-aided drafting equipment to produce designs, drawings, and charts. One of Sean's preferred career interests is hands-on.

Option 5: This choice is correct. An illustrator is classified as an artistic occupation. This is one of Sean's preferred career interests. As a person drawn to creative activities, such as visual art, Sean is interested in artistic careers.

Option 6: Correct. A multimedia designer is classified as an artistic occupation, which is one of Sean's preferred career interests. Multimedia designers use conceptual, technical, and visual design skills to create multimedia applications.

Sean's career values are artistic creativity and independence. Sean's preferred career interests are artistic and hands-on. Therefore, when selecting occupations, Sean should consider artistic professions with a hands-on dimension, such as graphic designer, illustrator, or multimedia designer.

Assessing your own career interests helps you zero in on appropriate occupations. Without such an assessment, it is very difficult to select an occupation when you have thousands to choose from.

Job skills that motivate you are also important to include in the career assessment section. Job skills make up the expertise needed to effectively perform a given job. Examples of job skills include planning meeting agendas, selling products, negotiating deals, and defining performance standards.

To create your list of job skills, you can include the skills you have acquired in former occupations and positions with other companies and volunteer work. Also include the skills you want to improve, and the skills you're interested in attaining.

Next, determine which skills you are interested in using. After you've written down all these job skills, decide which ones interest you the most.

Do this by ranking the job skills in order of preference. You may have already narrowed the list of occupations you're interested in, so your ranking should include the skills required for your chosen occupation. These skills should be ranked high; if not, you should consider pursuing another occupation.

Paul, the technical support engineer, gets the most job fulfillment from interfacing with customers. He also delights in resolving technical issues. Paul gets satisfaction from supporting team members with their support incidents.

Because Paul is in his element when helping others solve technical problems, he is less interested in working alone to analyze and test software. Nonetheless, he enjoys it in short stretches.

Case Study: Question 1 of 4
Scenario:

Doing Business Professionally

You've become increasingly dissatisfied with your position as a computer programmer. To identify your career values, career interests, and job skills, you're completing the career assessment section of a learning plan.

Answer the following questions in order.

Question:
What did you list as your career values?

Options:
1. profit
2. advancement
3. customer focus
4. change
5. independence
6. accomplishment

Answer:
Option 1: This choice is correct. You seek a profession that allows for limitless earning potential. You're interested in a field that places no limits on your earnings.

Option 2: This choice is incorrect. There is no indication that career advancement is one of your core professional principles. Having clear, attainable opportunities for advancement is not a motivating factor for you.

Option 3: This option is correct. You get satisfaction from pleasing and satisfying customers. You will work overtime to make sure customer expectations are met.

Option 4: This option is correct. You would like a job that allows for a frequent change of venues and tasks.

Option 5: This choice is incorrect. Independence is not necessarily one of your career values. Although you resist being controlled by others, there is no indication that you prefer working without significant direction from others.

Option 6: This choice is incorrect. There is no indication that accomplishment is one of your career values. You aren't necessarily motivated by the satisfaction of completing a difficult assignment properly.

Case Study: Question 2 of 4

What is your preferred career interest?

Options:

1. hands-on
2. social
3. enterprising
4. scientific
5. conventional

Answer:

Option 1: This option is not correct. Although you enjoy working with computers, you prefer working with people. Hands-on people prefer working primarily with tools, equipment, or machines.

Option 2: This choice is not correct. Although you enjoy working with people, you don't perceive yourself as a helper. Rather, you

prefer leading and persuading people, and selling products and ideas.

Option 3: This option is correct. As an enterprising person, you enjoy leading and persuading people, and selling things and ideas.

Option 4: This choice is not correct. People whose career interests are scientific typically avoid leading, selling, or persuading. You actually find these activities to be rewarding.

Option 5: This option is not correct. You dislike confining schedules and environments, and you avoid routine, detailed tasks. People whose career interests are conventional enjoy routine and structure.

Case Study: Question 3 of 4

Given your preferred career interests, which occupations are you most interested in pursuing?

Options:
1. computer support specialist
2. computer operator
3. software engineer
4. IT project director
5. software trainer
6. software sales representative

Answer:

Option 1: This option is not correct. Computer support specialists provide technical assistance, support, and advice to customers and other users. This is a social occupation; it is not an enterprising occupation.

Option 2: This choice is incorrect. Computer operator is a conventional occupation. Computer operators oversee the operation of computer hardware systems, ensuring that these machines are used as efficiently as possible.

Option 3: This choice is incorrect. Software engineer is a scientific occupation. Software engineers develop algorithms and analyze and solve programming problems.

Option 4: This option is correct. IT project director is classified as an enterprising occupation; it requires the ability to lead and motivate project team members to produce quality work and meet deadlines.

Option 5: This choice is incorrect. Software trainer is classified as a social profession. Your preference is an enterprising occupation.

Option 6: This choice is correct. Software sales representative is an enterprising occupation; it requires the ability to lead and persuade customers in order to sell software products.

Case Study: Question 4 of 4

You've chosen software sales representative and IT project director as the occupations you're most interested in pursuing. Which job skills are you most interested in using?

Options:

1. leading and persuading people, selling computer software, and providing customers with services
2. installing and repairing computer software
3. writing, testing, and maintaining software programs

Answer:

Option 1: This choice is correct. The job skills you're most interested in using at work are your problem-solving, interpersonal, and persuasive skills. You are also interested in providing customers with

software solutions.

Option 2: This is an incorrect choice. Although you have the ability to install and repair computer software, you have little interest in using these job skills.

Option 3: This choice is not correct. Though your technical skills include computer programming and software development, these are not skills you're interested in using.

Completing the career assessment section of a learning plan allowed you to discover your career values, your career interests, and the job skills that motivate you. This information revealed that software sales is a better fit for you.

Had you not completed the career assessment section, you would not have identified a more satisfying professional direction than computer programming.

Learning more about your career values, your career interests, and the job skills that appeal to you will help you identify your learning needs. And that's the first step toward knowing where you're going.

EFFECTIVE LEARNING OBJECTIVES FOR A SPECIFIC GOAL

Effective learning objectives for a specific goal

How would you define the word "objective"? A goal is the end to which you direct your efforts.

Objectives are often used to help people reach their goals. For the lifelong learner, an objective is often known as a learning objective. Learning objectives are statements that explain exactly what the learner will be able to do at the conclusion of instructional activities.

Lifelong learners apply learning objectives to their learning plan after they have identified the specific skills, knowledge, and abilities they want to acquire or enhance.

These learning objectives become the building blocks for reaching their goals.

The second section of a learning plan--career focus--centers around your goals and the learning objectives that will help you achieve them. An effective learning objective should:

- pertain to its corresponding goal,

- explain what skill, knowledge, or ability you will have upon its completion.

As you just learned, an effective learning objective should pertain to its corresponding goal. It should be framed in such a way that it's a required step in reaching a goal.

Select each objective type to discover what an effective and ineffective objective would be for the goal to become a project manager.

Effective objective

An effective learning objective for becoming a project manager is, "I will create project schedules and budgets using project management software."

Ineffective objective

An ineffective learning objective for becoming a project manager is, "I will be able to use web design software to create web pages."

An effective learning objective also explains what skill, knowledge, or ability you will have upon its completion. The objective must be more specific than vague, and more narrow than broad. But, it can't be too specific, because that will take it down to task level. A task is a concrete, measurable event.

Select each objective type for examples of creating effective learning objectives for the goal to become a project manager.

Effective objective

An effective learning objective for becoming a project manager is, "I will receive certification in project management." This objective states what you will have when you complete your educational pursuits.

Ineffective objective

An ineffective learning objective for becoming a project manager is, "I will learn all I can about managing projects." This objective is too broad and does not state what you will be able to do when you complete your educational pursuits.

Charlotte is a business analyst with a consulting firm. Her goal is to become a senior associate in nine months. One of the jobs of a senior associate is to make weekly presentations to clients; another is to lead a team.

Review the learning objectives and determine which ones are effective. Then review each objective to find out whether your observations are correct.

I will organize and deliver professional client presentations.

This objective is effective because it pertains to Charlotte's goal and explains what skills she will have upon its completion. In order to become a senior associate, Charlotte must be a skilled presenter.

I will improve my presentation skills.

Although this objective pertains to Charlotte's goal, it does not explain exactly what skill, knowledge, or ability Charlotte will have upon its completion.

I will effectively facilitate team meetings.

This objective is effective because it pertains to Charlotte's goal and explains what skills she will have upon its completion. To become a senior associate, Charlotte must be able to effectively facilitate team meetings.

I will work with my mentor to develop skills in research techniques.

This objective is ineffective because it does not explain what skill, knowledge, or ability Charlotte will have upon its completion. The objective also does not pertain to Charlotte's goal of becoming a senior associate. She does not need research skills as a senior associate.

I will go the extra mile in demonstrating my initiative at work.

This objective is ineffective because it is too broad, and doesn't pertain to Charlotte's goal. The objective doesn't explain exactly what skill, knowledge, or ability Charlotte will have upon its completion.

Question

Patty, an administrative assistant for a gas and electric company, likes using computers, but she's had no formal computer training. She volunteers as a lab monitor in the company's computer lab, where she provides technical support and helps employees understand the software programs used throughout the company. She wants to offer formal computer training classes. Select the examples of effective learning objectives for her goal to offer formal computer training classes.

Options:

1. I will become certified to teach classes for the pertinent programs.

2. I will do whatever it takes to hold formal computer training classes.

3. I will gain expert status in my company's word processing and spreadsheet software.

4. I will talk to my boss to find out how I can become the head of the computer lab.

Answer:

Option 1: This option is correct. This particular learning objective pertains to Patty's goal and explains what skill she will have upon its completion.

Option 2: This option is incorrect. Even though this learning objective pertains to Patty's goal to offer formal computer training classes, it is too broad. It also doesn't state what skill Patty will have upon its completion.

Option 3: Correct. This particular learning objective pertains to Patty's goal to offer formal computer training classes and explains what skills she will have upon its completion. She will have expert status in two computer applications.

Option 4: This option is incorrect. This learning objective does not pertain to Patty's goal to offer formal computer training classes.

When constructed correctly, your learning objectives will help you achieve your learning goals.

FORMULATING A LEARNING STRATEGY AND MEANS FOR EVALUATION

Formulating a learning strategy and means for evaluation

Imagine you've identified your learning needs, determined your learning goals, and constructed the appropriate learning objectives. All you need to do now is achieve those objectives, right?

In fact, you need to develop a learning strategy and a way to evaluate the learning objectives you've set. The last two sections of your learning plan will allow you to do just that.

A learning plan is a written road map for initiating and continuing career and professional development. The last two sections of a learning plan are named learning strategy and means for evaluation.

These last two sections are very important because they will:
- focus your efforts,
- ensure your accountability.

Jack, a copywriter in an advertising agency, was ready for a career change. After completing the career assessment and career focus sections of his learning plan, he knew that he wanted to be a teacher.

Jack's learning strategies and means for evaluation allowed him to focus his efforts. He listed each task, its resources, and its completion date.

His means for evaluation ensured his accountability. Jack wrote down the questions he was accountable for in regard to each task. His criteria were mainly, "Was it done?" and, "Was it done on time?"

Question

Select the reasons why it's important to formulate a learning strategy and means for evaluation.

Formulating a learning strategy and means for evaluation is important because they will...

Options:

1. focus my efforts on constructive tasks that will help me attain my learning objectives.

2. allow me to establish criteria by which to evaluate my learning plan.

3. assure that my learning objectives will result in professional satisfaction.

4. ensure that I am accountable for achieving my learning objectives.

5. help me establish my learning goals and objectives.

Answer:

Option 1: This is correct. Formulating learning strategies by listing tasks, resources, and completion dates will allow you to focus your efforts. You will create a road map for initiating and continuing career and professional development.

Option 2: This option is incorrect. Formulating a learning strategy and means for evaluation does not establish criteria for evaluating your learning plan. Rather, it enables you to evaluate your learning objectives.

Option 3: This choice is incorrect. Formulating a learning strategy and means for evaluation will not necessarily guarantee professional satisfaction. Many factors contribute to professional satisfaction.

Option 4: This choice is correct. Creating a learning strategy and means for evaluation for each learning objective will ensure accountability. You will have a plan for carrying out each learning objective.

Option 5: This choice is incorrect. In fact, the opposite is true. Your learning goals and objectives will allow you to establish your learning strategy and means for evaluation.

THE LEARNING STRATEGY SECTION OF A LEARNING PLAN

The learning strategy section of a learning plan

How will you go about attaining new skills or improving existing ones to achieve your professional dreams?

Successful lifelong learners know that after developing their learning objectives, they should develop a learning strategy for each objective.

The three steps for completing the learning strategy section of a learning plan are:

1. listing the tasks that compose each objective,

2. identifying the learning resources required for each task,

3. choosing a realistic target completion date for each task.

The first step is to list the tasks that compose each objective. A task is an action that must occur if objectives are to be achieved. To be effective, a task should be concrete and specific. Describe how you plan to carry out the task and what process you plan to follow to accomplish your objective. When tasks must be performed in succession, list them sequentially.

For example, tasks could include reading and studying, conducting interviews, performing experiments, taking a course, and researching.

A task may be something specific like writing a report, or it may be something general like getting information. If your task seems too broad, describe it in such a way that it becomes specific.

For example, instead of writing, "I will get information about degree programs," break it up to form two specific actions.

See each task to learn how to break up the task.

Task 1

I will generate a list of questions about degree programs.

Task 2

I will visit the web sites of the three colleges in my area to discover the answers to my questions.

Question

Linda is an employee relations specialist. Her learning objective is to become certified in mediation. To support her learning objective, she plans to learn more about mediation certification programs. Select the correct examples of tasks for Linda's learning objective.

Options:

1. I will gather information about mediation programs.

2. I will create a list of questions to ask when I contact mediation programs.

3. I will contact mediators to generate recommendations for mediation certification programs.

4. I will create a list of the most highly recommended mediation certification programs in my area. 5. I will determine which mediation program is the best.

Answer:

Option 1: This choice is not correct. This task is too broad. It needs to be broken down into specific actions.

Option 2: Correct. Creating a list of questions is a concrete, specific action that will help Linda reach her objective of becoming certified in mediation. This will prepare her for her phone calls with representatives from mediation programs.

Option 3: This is a correct choice. This task is framed in such a way that it is concrete and specific. Contacting mediators for recommendations are specific actions that will help Linda reach her objective of becoming certified in mediation.

Option 4: This choice is correct. This is written in such a way that the task is concrete. Creating a list is a specific action that will help Linda reach her objective of becoming certified in mediation.

Option 5: This option is not correct. This task is neither concrete nor specific.

The second step is to identify the learning resources required for each task. Learning resources are the people you plan to consult and the tools you plan to use to help you acquire the desired skill, knowledge, or ability.

You can find learning resources internally, within your organization, and externally. Some examples of internal learning resources are in-house training workshops and company-sponsored seminars, online training courses, and certification programs.

Doing Business Professionally

Additional examples include mentors, coworkers, vendors, and suppliers. You can also learn from challenging projects for which you can volunteer, such as laboratory trials and field experience.

External learning resources include formal academic courses and programs; teachers and instructors; professional association involvement, including conferences, monthly meetings, and networking events with other professionals in your field; books; manuals; and a variety of learning technologies, including computers and the Internet.

Question

Internal and external resources are the people you plan to consult and the tools you plan to use to help you accomplish a task.

Match each learning resources category to one or more appropriate examples.

Options:

A. internal learning resources

B. external learning resources

Targets:

1. instructor-led training for people seeking systems administrator certification

2. night classes to finish a master's degree

3. a lunch session on the use of spreadsheets

4. a week-long symposium to learn new techniques in medical research

5. a computer with Internet access

Answer:

Instructor-led training for people seeking systems administrator certification is an example of an external learning resource. Many commercial companies offer

163

instructor-led and online courses for specific certification programs.

Taking night classes to finish a master's degree is an example of an external learning resource. A master's degree program typically requires taking formal academic courses at a local university.

A lunch session on how to use spreadsheets is an example of an internal learning resource. It is an informal in-house training workshop.

A week-long symposium to learn new techniques in medical research is an example of an external learning resource. It is an event sponsored by a professional association.

A computer with Internet access is an example of an internal learning resource. It is a tool that you can use to acquire desired skills, knowledge, or abilities.

The third step is to choose a realistic target completion date for each task. Realistic means that you allow yourself enough time to perform your regular job duties when setting a target completion date. However, you should not set the date so far in the future that you forget about it.

Realistic also means that you don't set a date that's at the same time as a work deadline. Some target completion dates will already be set for you by external factors, such as application deadlines and conference dates.

Linda, the employee relations specialist, is involved in a demanding employee relations project that

begins today, January 15, with a deadline of March 1. She and her team members expect to work ten- hour days for six weeks prior to the deadline.

Despite this project, she wants to move forward with her learning strategy. Linda plans to start working on her learning strategy on February 1.

See each task and date to learn more about realistic and unrealistic completion dates for specific tasks.

Task 1

"I will create a list of questions to ask when I contact mediation programs."

February 3

A target completion date of February 3 for creating a list of questions for mediation programs is unrealistic. Because Linda is involved in a demanding employee relations project, she must give herself more time for such a task.

February 20

A target completion date of February 20 is realistic because it gives Linda enough time to complete the task, especially given her demanding workload. It is also not so far ahead that she will forget about the task.

Task 2

"I will contact mediators to generate recommendations for mediation certification programs."

March 10

A target completion date of March 10 is realistic. It gives Linda enough time to complete the task, given her deadline on March 1. This date is not so far ahead that she will forget about the task.

April 15

A target completion date of April 15 is too far ahead for this task. If Linda were to establish this date as the target completion date, she would run the risk of forgetting about the task.

Task 3
"I will create a list of recommended mediation certification programs in my area."

March 1

A target completion date of March 1 is unrealistic; this task must be performed after Linda contacts mediators. Also, this is the same date as the employee relations project deadline, an important deadline for Linda's work.

March 15

A target completion date of March 15 is realistic; it gives Linda enough time to complete both the task and her project responsibilities.

Question

Charlotte, a business analyst, is involved in a project where she and her team are coordinating the development of market research studies in support of strategic planning, and presenting findings to clients. The current date is May 1, and the final client presentation is scheduled for May 10. Charlotte would like to make progress on her learning objective to work with a mentor to develop team leadership skills. Her first task is to select a mentor. What is a realistic target completion date for this task?

Options:
1. May 5
2. May 10
3. June 1
4. July 15

Answer:

Option 1: This option is incorrect. This target completion date does not allow Charlotte enough time to perform her regular job duties.

Option 2: This choice is not correct. This target completion date is the same date as Charlotte's final client presentation. Therefore, this is not a realistic target completion date.

Option 3: This choice is correct. This target completion date is realistic in that it gives Charlotte enough time to perform her regular job duties and is not so far ahead that she risks forgetting about the task.

Option 4: This option is incorrect. This target completion date is so far in the future that Charlotte may forget about the task.

The three steps for completing the learning strategy section of a learning plan are to sequentially list the tasks that compose each objective, to identify the learning resources required for each task, and to choose a realistic target completion date for each task.

If one of the three steps is inconclusive or missing altogether, the learning strategy will not be effective in helping you meet your learning objective.

Question

On December 15, Owen moved into his new position as office manager at his company. He was an administrative assistant prior to taking this position. His learning objective is to learn his company's policies and procedures by reading the company's manual. Select the effective learning strategy.

Options:

1. I will read one section of the manual each week, beginning the week of January 1. I will meet with my supervisor every Monday morning to report what I learned and to ask any questions I may have. I will finish the task by February 1.

2. I will read one section of the manual each week. I will meet with my supervisor every Monday morning to report what I learned and to ask any questions I may have.

3. I will read one section of the manual each week beginning the week of January 1. I will finish the task by February 1.

Answer:

Option 1: This choice is correct. Owen has listed the tasks that compose his objective and identified the learning resources required for each task. He has also chosen a realistic target completion date for the tasks.

Option 2: This is an incorrect choice. This learning strategy is incomplete; there is no target completion date for the tasks.

Option 3: This option is incorrect. In this case, Owen has not listed all of his tasks. To create an effective learning strategy, he must do so.

It's important that you address all three steps for completing an effective learning strategy. The three steps are:

1. listing the tasks that compose each objective,
2. identifying the learning resources required for each task,
3. choosing a realistic target completion date for each task.

To determine what tasks you must perform to carry out your objective, identify the measurable events that must occur if the objective is to be achieved. Create a flowchart or a list in which you write the required tasks.

If one task relies on another, then list those tasks sequentially. If tasks are sequential, document the step-by-step instructions for performing the process. Ask yourself, "What should I do first, second, third, and so on?"

Colleen is a project manager whose goal is to attain project management professional (PMP) certification. In talking to a senior project manager at work, she learned about the process she should follow to attain PMP certification.

The senior project manager recommended that Colleen take a PMP certification exam preparation course and use the strategies taught and materials distributed in the course to prepare for the exam.

One of Colleen's objectives is to satisfy the Project Management Institute's Continuing Certification Requirements Program. Her other objective is to pass the PMP examination, scheduled for May 25. She is constructing a learning strategy for the latter learning objective. Colleen will be busy at work until April 30. Her first step is to sequentially list the tasks that compose this objective.

See each task in order, to learn more about how Colleen lists the tasks.

Task 1: Course Selection
"I will select and register for a web-based self-study PMP certification exam preparation course."

Task 2: Course Completion
"I will complete a web-based self-study PMP certification exam preparation course."

Task 3: Exam Preparation
"I will prepare for the PMP certification exam."

Task 4: Exam Completion
"I will take the PMP certification exam."

Next, to complete the second step of formulating a learning strategy, you have to consider the tasks one at a time.

For each task, ask yourself, "What resources do I need to help me carry out this task?" Determine whether you must consult an institution, an expert, a professional organization, a written document, or a web resource.

Colleen consulted a senior project manager at work to identify the required learning resources. She has completed the second step by identifying the learning resources required for each of the tasks that compose her learning objective.

See each task to discover the learning resources associated with the tasks Colleen listed.

Task 1: course selection

"In order to select a PMP certification exam preparation course, I will contact my local Project Management Institute chapter, post the question to project management mailing lists on the Internet, and visit various project management web sites."

Task 2: course completion

"I will use my laptop and the course provider's web site to take the self-study PMP certification exam preparation course."

Task 3: exam preparation

"To prepare for the PMP certification exam, I will study the Project Management Institute's book, 'A Guide to the Project Management Body of Knowledge' and course materials."

Task 4: exam completion

"I will take the PMP certification exam at a local testing center."

To perform the third step, ask yourself, "What is a realistic target completion date for each task?" Set a realistic target completion date for each task by considering your work demands and pertinent deadlines.

Determine the exact or approximate time required to complete the task. Don't set a date on the same day as a due date you have at work.

Colleen's PMP examination is scheduled for May 25. She will be busy at work until April 30. She has set realistic target completion dates for each of her tasks.

See the tasks and target completion dates to learn more.

Course selection

"I will select and register for a web-based self-study PMP certification exam preparation course."

May 1

"My target completion date for selecting a PMP exam preparation course is May 1. Although I will be very busy until April 30, a month is enough time to conduct research on various PMP preparation courses."

Course completion

"I will complete a web-based self-study PMP certification exam preparation course."

May 11

"A web-based self-study PMP certification exam preparation course will take 20 hours to complete. I would like to complete the course two weeks before the test. I will start the course on May 3 and finish by May 11."

Exam preparation

"I will prepare for the PMP certification exam."

May 24

"I will complete my PMP certification exam preparation on May 24, the day before the exam on May 25."

Exam completion

"I will take the PMP certification exam."

May 25

"I will take the PMP certification exam on May 25."

One of Colleen's objectives was to pass the PMP certification examination. Her planning process was shaped by the fact that she had registered to take the exam on May 25. Three of the tasks relied on another task, so Colleen listed those tasks sequentially. Colleen also had to factor in her work demands.

Had Colleen not mapped out her learning strategy in this way, she may have overcommitted herself and not allotted enough time for exam preparation. She could have failed the exam and have been required to repeat the process.

Case Study: Question 1 of 3

Scenario

You have become increasingly dissatisfied with your position as a computer programmer. Although you enjoy working with computers, you've realized that programming is not right for you. You dislike the isolation and the fixed salary. Your goal is to become a solution specialist with a company that specializes in web conferencing and web-collaboration software. A company in this field contacted you and scheduled a job interview on October 19; the company gave you two weeks' lead time. Your objective is to put together a sales presentation for your interview. To do so, you must learn as much as possible about the company's web conferencing and web-collaboration software. You will use the software to create your presentation. You must balance your interview preparation with a project that wraps up on October 7. Create a learning strategy for your objective.

Question

What will the first part of your learning strategy include?

Sequence the tasks.

Options:

A. I will select a web seminar on conferencing and web-collaboration software to attend.

B. I will attend a web seminar on conferencing and web-collaboration software.

C. I will purchase the conferencing and web-collaboration software.

D. I will practice using the software and explore all its features.

E. I will prepare a sales presentation using the software.

Answer:

I will select a web seminar on conferencing and web-collaboration software to attend. is ranked the first task in the learning strategy - This is the first task of the objective to put together a sales presentation for your interview. You must first select a web seminar as an introduction to the web-collaboration software.

I will attend a web seminar on conferencing and web-collaboration software. is ranked the second task in the learning strategy - This is the second task of the objective to put together a sales presentation for your interview. After selecting a seminar, you will attend the seminar. This task will give you the information you need to be able to purchase and use the software.

I will purchase the conferencing and web-collaboration software. is ranked the third task in the learning strategy - This is the third task of the objective to put together a sales presentation for your interview. Once you have attended the web seminar, you will purchase the conferencing and web-collaboration software.

I will practice using the software and explore all its features. is ranked the fourth task in the learning strategy - This is the fourth task of the objective to put together a sales presentation for your interview. After purchasing the software, you will use it and explore all its features. Becoming familiar with the software will allow you to prepare your presentation.

I will prepare a sales presentation using the software. is ranked the fifth task in the learning strategy - This is the fifth task of your objective. Because this task relies on the four previous tasks, the tasks must be performed sequentially.

Case Study: Question 2 of 3

What will the next part of your learning strategy include?

Options:

1. conferencing and web-collaboration software,
2. presentation software,
3. a computer with Internet access.

Answer:

Option 1: This option is correct. Conferencing and web-collaboration software is required for your presentation.

Option 2: This choice is incorrect. You will use conferencing and web-collaboration software for your presentation, not presentation software.

Option 3: This choice is correct. In order to attend a web seminar on conferencing and web- collaboration software, you must have a computer with Internet access.

Case Study: Question 3 of 3

Select the answer that correctly identifies the target completion date.

You will attend the web seminar by which date?

Options:
1. October 5
2. October 7
3. October 12
4. October 17
5. October 19

Answer:

Option 1: This option is not correct. This is not a realistic target completion date because it does not give you enough time to select and register for the web seminar while performing your regular job duties.

Option 2: This option is incorrect. This is not a realistic target completion date because it does not allow you enough time to perform your regular job duties.

Option 3: This choice is correct. This target completion date gives you enough time to perform your regular job duties, complete the web seminar, and prepare your presentation for your interview.

Option 4: This choice is not correct. This date does not give you enough time to complete the web seminar and prepare your presentation for your interview.

Option 5: This is an incorrect choice. You must complete the seminar before your interview.

You developed a learning strategy for the objective to put together a sales presentation for your interview. You did this by completing the learning strategy section of a learning plan.

First you sequentially listed the tasks that compose each objective. Then you identified the learning resources required for the tasks. Finally you chose a realistic target completion date for one of the tasks.

By following the three steps, you were able to find your way for achieving your goal of becoming a solution specialist. Take the time to complete the learning strategy section of your learning plan. It is the most detailed part of the road map you develop for achieving your professional dreams.

MEANS FOR EVALUATION

Means for evaluation

No learning strategy is complete if it doesn't include a way for you to verify whether you have accomplished each task.

In many learning plans, this information is contained in the fourth section: means for evaluation. A learning plan is a written road map for initiating and continuing career and professional development.

In the means for evaluation section, you will describe the method you'll use to determine whether you have accomplished your tasks successfully.

The strategies for correctly completing the means for evaluation section of a learning plan are: • reporting your progress to another stakeholder

• verifying whether you completed the task

• verifying that you met the target date for completion.

One strategy for correctly completing the means for evaluation section is to report your progress to another stakeholder who will be affected by your decision to become a lifelong learner.

A stakeholder could be a supervisor, a mentor, a coworker, a life coach, a career counselor, a team leader, your spouse, or a family member.

If one of your learning goals pertains to the company you're already working for, talk with your supervisor about your learning plan.

See the actions for more information.

Review

Go over your plan in detail with your supervisor. Ask her to help you remain accountable for accomplishing your tasks.

Report

For example, ask her whether she would meet with you the day after each deadline for a task so you can report on its status and ask her any questions you may have.

If your goal is to change careers, then in most cases it's probably inappropriate to consider your current supervisor as a stakeholder. It could be appropriate, though, if you have a close relationship with your supervisor.

Another strategy for establishing means for evaluation is to verify whether you completed the task. If your task is measurable, your criteria must measure the outcome.

Measurable means that the task has verifiable criteria for its success. For example, if your task is to receive 90 percent or higher on an exam, your exam score will be your measurable evaluation criterion.

You can also verify completion of tasks with items that signify completion, such as a certificate from a completed course or training session.

Your evaluation criteria must support your learning objective. For example, imagine you are deciding on a field of medicine to pursue. Your learning objective is to select a specialty, and one of your associated tasks is to conduct interviews with doctors in different specialty areas.

See each of the evaluation criteria to find out if it would be appropriate for this task.

completed six interviews with doctors

This evaluation criterion is not appropriate because it does not support your learning objective: to select a specialty.

completed interviews with doctors in six different specialty areas of medicine

This evaluation criterion is appropriate. Because you are deciding which area of medicine to pursue, it's imperative that you interview doctors who specialize in different areas.

The last strategy is to verify that you met the target date for completion. If you complete your task by the target date you established for the task, you have met this criterion.

For example, if your goal is to become a published author, and your objective is to submit a magazine article for publication, then one of your tasks might be to complete an article for submission by August 9.

In this case, August 9 would be your target date for completion. By August 10, you would have to verify whether you completed this task.

Colleen, a project manager with a telecommunications company, recently attained her project management professional (PMP) certification. Her goal is to become a senior project manager at a software company. One of her objectives is to land five interviews. Colleen has a formal relationship with her boss.

See each task and observation to learn how Colleen completed the means for evaluation section of her learning plan.

Task 1

"I'll create a resume and cover letter that highlight my PMP certification and detail my project management experience. I'll start developing my resume and cover letter on May 1."

Observation (Task 1)

Colleen's task does not contain evaluation criteria. She doesn't have a plan to report her progress on resume and cover letter development to another stakeholder, nor does she have a plan for verifying the task. Colleen is also missing a target date for completion.

Task 2

"I'll ask my boss to help me stay accountable for contacting ten potential employers each week by Thursday afternoon. I'll ask her to meet with me on Friday so that I can give her a status report."

Observation (Task 2)

Colleen's task contains inappropriate evaluation criteria. Her boss is not an appropriate stakeholder for this objective. An appropriate choice would be a career counselor or mentor.

The errors displayed by Colleen on the previous page could adversely affect her ability to measure her success.

This will ultimately affect her ability to achieve her learning objective, to schedule interviews, and her learning goal to get a new position as a senior project manager.

Doing Business Professionally

As you complete your learning tasks, remember to evaluate their outcomes. Doing so will ensure you're on the right track to achieving your learning objectives, and ultimately, attaining your learning goals.

WORKING WITH A MENTOR

Working with a mentor

Take a minute to think back over your life. Does anyone stand out as being particularly helpful or insightful? Did anyone ever challenge you--in a way that bolstered your self-esteem--to work harder and become more proficient at something?

Some people remember one or two teachers, coaches, troop leaders, religious leaders, or college advisors who made a difference in their lives.

If you remember someone like this, that person was most likely your mentor, even if neither of you thought of him in those terms.

A mentor has a lot of experience and influence in a chosen field, and he uses it to help and guide another person's--the protege's--professional development.

A mentor can, but does not have to, work for the same organization that employs the protege.

Working with a mentor can be a valuable experience for you, no matter how old you are or what stage you're at in your career.

See each statement to learn more about the value of working with a mentor.

A mentor guides you as you develop and carry out your professional learning plan.

Your mentor should ask you questions and help you work through the answers so that you develop the right learning goals, learning objectives, and learning tasks to help you advance in your career and grow professionally.

A mentor can help you become adept as a lifelong learner.

After months of working with your mentor, you may begin to strive to learn more and become better on your own. This result could very well continue even after the official relationship with your mentor has ended.

A mentor allows you to examine your performance in a safe environment.

A mentor should offer you her objective opinions regarding your job performance. Because she is your champion and she wants you to succeed, you can listen to and follow up on her advice without feeling threatened.

Question

Now that you know how valuable it can be to work with a mentor, how comfortable are you with the idea of finding someone to guide you along your lifelong learning path?

Options:

1. not at all comfortable
2. not very comfortable
3. somewhat comfortable
4. pretty comfortable
5. extremely comfortable

Answer:

Option 1: People often find themselves overwhelmed by the time and effort it takes to establish and maintain their professional growth. A mentor can help moderate your stress and teach you how to use it to your advantage.

Option 2: People often find themselves overwhelmed by the time and effort it takes to establish and maintain their professional growth. A mentor can help moderate your stress and teach you how to use it to your advantage.

Option 3: People often find themselves overwhelmed by the time and effort it takes to establish and maintain their professional growth. A mentor can help moderate your stress and teach you how to use it to your advantage.

Option 4: People often find themselves overwhelmed by the time and effort it takes to establish and maintain their professional growth. A mentor can help moderate your stress and teach you how to use it to your advantage.

Option 5: People often find themselves overwhelmed by the time and effort it takes to establish and maintain their professional growth. A mentor can help moderate your stress and teach you how to use it to your advantage.

Question

Recognize the value of working with a mentor by selecting the statements that correctly complete the following sentence.

A mentor...

Options:

1. allows you to examine your performance in a safe environment.
2. ensures that you meet your performance objectives.
3. guides you as you develop and carry out your professional learning plan.
4. can help you become adept as a lifelong learner.

5. allows you to eliminate stress at work.
6. ensures professional advancement.

Answer:

Option 1: This choice is correct. A mentor should give you objective feedback about your job performance. As your advocate, she should promote your best interests. Therefore, you can take her advice without feeling threatened.

Option 2: This is an incorrect choice. A mentor can help you work toward your performance objectives, but he will not necessarily ensure that you meet your objectives. You are responsible for making sure that happens.

Option 3: This choice is correct. Your mentor should advise you to develop the right learning goals, learning objectives, and learning tasks to promote your career advancement and professional growth.

Option 4: This is a correct response. After working with your mentor, you may begin to strive to learn more and improve on your own. This may have long-lasting effects even after the official relationship with your mentor has ended.

Option 5: This is an incorrect response. A mentor will not necessarily enable you to eliminate stress at work, but she can help you moderate your stress and teach you how to use it to your advantage.

Option 6: This is an incorrect choice. A mentor will help you maintain professional growth, but he will not necessarily ensure professional advancement. Many other factors are at play in advancement decisions.

This lesson covers one of the potential learning resources that you might include in the learning strategy

section of your learning plan: working with a mentor. Specifically, you will learn what qualities:
- to look for in a mentor,
- you, the protege, should have to ensure a successful relationship with your mentor.

MENTOR QUALITIES

Mentor qualities

Imagine that you and several others have been shipwrecked on an island. Only one person in your group can speak the same language as the locals.

Like the island spokesperson, a mentor is a compassionate person who influences your fate. A mentor is someone with a great deal of experience and influence in a chosen field who helps and guides your-- the protege's--professional or career development.

A mentor can, but does not have to, work for the same organization that employs you.

An effective mentor possesses many qualities that allow him to help you develop professionally. If a mentor works for the same firm as you do, he should possess company-specific knowledge. An effective mentor is also:

- experienced
- dedicated
- influential
- credible
- insistent

- verbally adept
- good at listening
- objective
- encouraging

See each attribute to find out more about five of the ten desired qualities of an effective mentor.

in possession of company-specific knowledge

If a mentor works for the same organization as you, he should know how the organization functions, such as how to get things done and how to advance through the ranks. To be effective, your mentor must also be willing to share his company-specific knowledge.

experienced

An effective mentor is experienced and is willing to share his skills and expertise. Your mentor's skills and expertise should match your professional development needs and career goals.

dedicated

A mentor helps you achieve your learning goals. He should participate fully in the mentoring relationship. To show dedication, he must set clear expectations, define roles, determine meeting logistics, and decide how to deal with problems when they arise.

influential

A mentor should know people throughout the industry--and if applicable, throughout the organization--and be able to introduce you to the ones who can help you reach your learning goals.

credible

A mentor should be credible within the profession, and if applicable, the organization. His colleagues should respect him, his work, and his opinions.

Charlotte is a business analyst with a consulting firm. Her goal is to become a senior associate within nine months. One of the jobs of a senior associate is to make weekly presentations to clients; another is to lead a team.

Charlotte would like to make progress on her objective to work with a mentor to develop team leadership skills. She has asked Sam, a senior analyst, to be her mentor, and Sam has agreed to take on the role.

Follow along in a conversation where Sam is ineffective in mentoring Charlotte. In other words, Sam does not demonstrate the first five desired qualities here.

Charlotte: Do you have some ideas for working toward a senior associate position? Having been a senior associate yourself, and now a senior analyst, you have the skills and expertise I'm seeking. Can you give me insight into the organizational politics of our firm?

Sam: I know how things work around here, but after all these years, I like to keep a low profile and stay out of organizational politics. My advice to you is to take the path of least resistance.

Charlotte: I see. Well, I'm sure you have some valuable expertise to share with me. So, when and where would you like to meet, and what should our roles be?

Sam: I prefer an informal approach to mentoring. We can leave it open ended and meet whenever a need arises. I'll let you take the lead.

Charlotte: OK. Do you think you can help me connect with the senior partners who make the promotion decisions?

Sam: Perhaps. I'll see what I can do, but I think it's best for you to approach them yourself. That will demonstrate your proactive working style and make the best impression.

Charlotte: Do you have ideas for approaching some of the senior partners? Or can you set something up for me?

Sam: I'm not sure. Ever since we lost the RPJ account, I've felt that my relationship with some of the senior partners has become strained. But I'll see what I can do.

Sam did not display the qualities of an effective mentor in his interaction with Charlotte. As a result, it's likely that she felt frustrated and uncertain about the benefits she would receive from her mentoring relationship with Sam.

See each attribute to learn more about the qualities Sam could have demonstrated as he was mentoring Charlotte.

In possession of company-specific Knowledge

Although Sam possessed company-specific knowledge, he did not share it with Charlotte. Instead, he advised her to keep a low profile and stay out of organizational politics. Thus, his knowledge had no real value for Charlotte.

Experience

Sam's expertise matches Charlotte's professional development needs and career goals, but he was not necessarily willing to share his expertise with her. Instead, he advised her to keep a low profile.

Dedication

Sam failed to show dedication by not setting clear expectations with Charlotte. Instead, he told her that he preferred an informal approach. It's unlikely that Sam intends to prioritize his mentoring duties.

Influence

Sam appeared unwilling or unable to use his influence to help Charlotte reach her learning goals. He encouraged her to approach the senior partners herself.

Credibility

Sam's credibility appeared to be in question. He referred to strained relations between himself and some of the senior partners.

Follow along in a conversation where Sam demonstrates the first five qualities of an effective mentor with Charlotte.

Charlotte: Do you have some ideas for working toward a senior associate position? Having been a senior associate yourself, and now a senior analyst, you have the skills and expertise I'm seeking. Can you give me insight into the organizational politics of our firm?

Sam: Definitely. I can use my influence to help you position yourself as a strong candidate for the senior associate position. It's important to attend the networking events and take the lead on projects. That way, you're visible to the people who make the promotion decisions. I'll make sure you meet all the right people.

Sam: You should know that all of the business analysts I've recommended for senior associate positions have received promotions. I guess my opinion counts for something around here.

Charlotte: I'm sure it does, Sam. So, when and where would you like to meet, and how should we define our mentoring roles?

Sam: Let's meet in my office once a week on Fridays, at 3:00, to create a plan for working toward a senior associate position. That way we can assess your progress every week. Does that sound good?

Charlotte: It sounds perfect, Sam.

In the example on the previous page, Sam demonstrated the qualities of an effective mentor, which encouraged and motivated Charlotte.

See each attribute to learn more about the qualities Sam demonstrated as he was mentoring Charlotte.

in possession of company-specific knowledge

Sam shared his company-specific knowledge with Charlotte when he stressed the importance of attending networking events and taking the lead on projects. This information will help Charlotte as she works toward her goal of becoming a senior associate.

experienced

Sam's skills and expertise match Charlotte's professional development needs and career goals. He worked as a senior associate prior to becoming a senior analyst. His expertise and insights about his own career path will be invaluable to Charlotte.

dedicated

Sam demonstrated his dedication when he established parameters for his mentoring relationship with Charlotte. He set up a regular meeting time and proposed a plan of action.

influential

Sam demonstrated his pull when he told Charlotte he would use his influence to help her position herself for the job of senior associate. Sam promised Charlotte that he would introduce her to contacts who could potentially help her achieve her goal.

credible

When Sam told Charlotte that all the business analysts he had recommended for senior associate positions had been promoted, he demonstrated his credibility. Clearly, his colleagues value his opinions on promotion decisions.

See each attribute to learn more about the remaining five desired qualities a mentor should demonstrate.

insistent

A mentor should challenge you to reach beyond what is familiar and comfortable so you can grow from new experiences.

encouraging

A mentor should provide you with positive encouragement so that you'll be more willing to push yourself beyond your normal boundaries and work through the low spots in your efforts. Additionally, he should encourage you to expand upon your strengths.

objective

Your mentor is your champion; he wants you to succeed. To effectively assess your strengths and weaknesses, he needs to remain objective and not let feelings or prejudices get in the way. It's OK for your mentor to acknowledge your weaknesses, but he should not let bias be a factor.

verbally adept

A mentor should be able to communicate well verbally. His answers and feedback should be clear and concise, and he should be able to give you succinct, pertinent instructions and examples.

good at listening

A mentor should listen to what you are telling him about your needs and concerns. That way, the guidance he offers will be relevant to you.

Charlotte and Sam are discussing her objectives. Follow along in a conversation where Sam doesn't demonstrate the remaining five desired qualities.

Charlotte: In order to become a senior associate, I must develop my presentation skills. The only problem is that I have anxiety about speaking in front of groups.

Sam: Yeah, most women have that problem. Perhaps it's best that you avoid that task. It won't reflect well on our company if your client presentations don't go smoothly. If you're uncomfortable with the task of presenting to clients, you can ask another analyst to be the lead presenter.

Charlotte: Good idea. I prefer to let someone who is more skilled handle the client presentations. Thanks for your input. I know I should also become skilled at leading meetings. What should I know about facilitating team meetings?

Sam: Basically, it's important to plan for meetings. Then when you're facilitating meetings, you must pick up on group dynamics and lead the meeting accordingly.

Charlotte: I'm not clear how to approach these tasks. Can you give me some pointers?

Sam: You must observe the interpersonal interactions and intervene when necessary.

Charlotte: I guess I don't understand the point you're trying to make.

Sam: Don't worry, Charlotte, you'll be fine. Now, let's finish this client analysis.

Because Sam did not demonstrate the qualities of an effective mentor during their interaction, Charlotte most likely felt self-doubt and confusion.

See each attribute to learn more about the qualities that Sam could have demonstrated as he was mentoring Charlotte.

Insistent

Sam did not challenge Charlotte to reach beyond her comfort level and grow from new experiences. He encouraged her to avoid public speaking, a task that makes her uncomfortable.

Encouraging

Sam did not encourage Charlotte to push herself beyond her normal boundaries and work through the low spots in her efforts. In fact, he confirmed her fear that she lacked public speaking skills.

Objective

Sam did not stay objective when mentoring Charlotte. He introduced personal bias when assessing her public speaking skills.

Verbally Adept

Sam's answers, feedback, and instructions were vague and imprecise. Charlotte was unclear about his instructions for leading meetings.

A Good Listener

Sam didn't pick up on the need to explain strategies for leading team meetings. He didn't listen to what Charlotte was telling him about her needs and concerns. Instead, he was anxious to finish his task at hand.

Follow along in a conversation where Sam effectively mentors Charlotte as they discuss her objectives. Sam demonstrates the remaining five qualities.

Charlotte: In order to become a senior associate, I must develop my presentation skills. The only problem is, I have anxiety about speaking in front of groups.

Sam: Anxiety about public speaking is easy to overcome. It just takes practice. You have the poise, presence, and professionalism to be an excellent public speaker, Charlotte. Don't be too hard on yourself if you feel anxiety before your presentation. That's normal.

Charlotte: Thanks for your support. I suppose with practice, I'll learn to overcome the anxiety. I know I should also become skilled at leading meetings. What should I know about facilitating team meetings?

Sam: Leading team meetings requires an agenda, effective time management, strategies for encouraging participation, and a plan for follow up. You must also determine whether it is a decision-making, informational, or problem-solving meeting. I can help you develop these skills.

Charlotte: It sounds as though there's a lot to consider. How do you make sure you perform all the necessary activities?

Sam: You seem tentative about the task. Don't worry-- I've noticed that you're a gifted communicator. As we work together, we'll develop a plan to foster your meeting facilitation skills.

Charlotte: Great. I know I'm in good hands.

This time, Sam demonstrated the qualities of an effective mentor, which encouraged and motivated Charlotte and instilled confidence in her.

See each attribute to learn more about the qualities that Sam demonstrated as he was mentoring Charlotte.

insistent

Sam challenged Charlotte to reach beyond what is comfortable and to grow from new experiences. He demonstrated insistence when he told Charlotte that through practice, she could overcome her anxiety with public speaking.

encouraging

Sam encouraged Charlotte when he told her that she has the poise, presence, and professionalism to be an excellent public speaker. He encouraged Charlotte to push herself beyond her normal boundaries and to work through the low spots in her efforts.

objective

Sam demonstrated objectivity when he championed Charlotte without showing any preconceived notions about her public speaking skills. He also subtly acknowledged her anxiety without judging her.

verbally adept

Sam was verbally adept in his interaction with Charlotte. He provided feedback and answers that were clear and concise. When he explained meeting facilitation, he gave Charlotte succinct, pertinent instructions.

a good listener

Sam demonstrated his listening skills when he said he noticed that Charlotte was tentative about the task of meeting facilitation. He listened to Charlotte's concerns and offered relevant guidance.

Case Study: Question 1 of 2
Scenario

For your convenience, the case study is repeated with each question.

Dale, a training coordinator, has asked his boss, Sharon, to be his mentor. Sharon, the vice president of training and development, has agreed. In the past, Sharon has occasionally invited Dale to some of the company's executive meetings.

Follow along as Dale and Sharon meet to discuss professional development opportunities for Dale. Then answer the questions that follow, in order.

Dale: I really appreciate your inviting me to attend the management meetings. It has provided me with the opportunity to network with departmental managers.

Sharon: I recall when I was first starting out and was eager to learn as much as I could about the business. It would have been nice if someone had shown me the way. Now that I've established credibility with the management team and am in a leadership position, I enjoy coaching promising associates.

Dale: Well, I'm glad to hear you say that.

Sharon: Tell me, do you have any particular career aspirations?

Dale: Yes. Lately, I've been thinking of eventually becoming a training manager or director. Attending the management meetings has helped me understand company-wide training needs.

Sharon: You know, Dale, I believe you have potential for becoming a successful training director. That's why I decided to invite you to the management meetings. The more you network with managers, the better your chances of moving up when an opportunity arises.

Sharon: I'm happy to learn that you're interested in making training and development a long-term career. As it happens, an important training directive has come across my desk, and I've been trying to decide how to handle it. Do you think you'd be up for the job?

Dale: Certainly. I will gladly step up to the challenge, and I appreciate the confidence you have in my abilities. I look forward to working with you and learning from your expertise about the field.

Question

What are the other desired mentor qualities that Sharon demonstrated?

Options:

1. experienced
2. influential
3. credible
4. insistent
5. verbally adept

Answer:

Option 1: This is correct. As the vice president of training and development, Sharon's skills and expertise match Dale's professional development needs and career goals. He hopes to advance from a training coordinator to a training director.

Option 2: This choice is correct. Sharon regularly attends management meetings, and she is in a position to introduce Dale to managers who can help him reach his goals.

Option 3: This option is correct. As vice president of training and development, Sharon is a leader in her organization. Her colleagues respect her and her input.

Option 4: This option is correct. Sharon challenged Dale to reach beyond his comfort level and grow from new experiences by offering him a new training assignment.

Option 5: This option is incorrect. Sharon did not demonstrate verbal adeptness. She didn't give Dale succinct, pertinent instructions and examples. Rather, she provided vague directives.

Case Study: Question 2 of 2

What are some of the desired mentor qualities that Sharon demonstrated?

Options:

1. encouraging
2. in possession of company-specific knowledge
3. good at listening
4. dedicated
5. compassionate

Answer:

Option 1: Correct. When Sharon told Dale that she believed he had the potential for becoming a successful training director, she was providing encouragement to Dale so that he would be more willing to push himself beyond his normal boundaries.

Option 2: This choice is correct. As a member of the management team, Sharon is familiar with the inner workings of the organization, knows how to get things done, and understands how to advance through the ranks.

Option 3: This option is correct. Sharon listened to what Dale told her about his professional needs and concerns. By listening to his aspirations, she was able to offer guidance that was relevant to Dale.

Option 4: This choice is not correct. Although Sharon agreed to be Dale's mentor, she did not set expectations with him, such as defining mentoring roles and making logistical arrangements for regular meeting times.

Option 5: This option is incorrect. Being compassionate is not one of the explicitly stated desired mentor qualities.

By demonstrating many of the qualities of an effective mentor, Sharon encouraged Dale to stretch himself professionally. Her listening skills enabled her to offer relevant guidance. Sharon's experience, influence, credibility, and company-specific knowledge will help Dale reach his professional goals.

If Sharon had failed to demonstrate the qualities of an effective mentor, it is likely that Dale would feel self-doubt, confusion, and frustration. He might also question the benefits to be gained from his mentoring relationship with Sharon.

It's difficult to chart the best course for your professional development and learning needs. A mentor can reduce some of that difficulty and offer you valuable guidance.

PROTEGE QUALITIES

Protege qualities

Have you ever been in a relationship where you feel as though the other person is always calling the shots? If so, how did that make you feel? Did you ever do anything that you wanted to do?

Mentoring offers you the opportunity to accept guidance and input from an expert in your field; it should not entail handing over complete control of your professional life.

Entering into a mentoring relationship is just like entering into any other type of relationship: both parties have to work to ensure that the relationship results in a win-win situation. An effective protege is:
- dedicated
- adaptable
- persistent
- responsible

A protege should take the time and expend the effort necessary to achieve his learning goals. He should be an active participant in the mentoring relationship; after all, it's his professional development at stake.

See each attribute to learn about the qualities of an effective protege.

Dedicated

To be dedicated, a protege should take time to achieve his learning goals. Showing dedication includes setting clear expectations with the mentor, defining roles, determining meeting logistics, and deciding how to deal with problems when they arise.

Adaptable

A mentor is a busy professional who is donating valuable time to the protege. To be adaptable, the protege should be willing to reschedule appointments and accept that meetings may be interrupted occasionally.

Responsible

A responsible protege prepares for a meeting with his mentor. Before the meeting, he should provide a list of carefully considered and professional questions to maximize the use of the mentor's time. If that's not possible, he should bring the list to the meeting.

Persistent

Because a mentor is a professional with many demands, she may tend to put other priorities ahead of the protege more often than she should. The protege should be persistent in asking for the amount of time he needs to spend with the mentor.

To show dedication, you should establish clear expectations with your mentor by defining the roles and logistics of your mentoring relationship. Without taking the time to establish parameters and ground rules, you may not achieve the learning goals you set for your mentoring relationship.

As the protege, you must be adaptable--willing to reschedule appointments and accept that meetings may be interrupted. If you demonstrate inflexibility to your mentor, he may lose interest in working with you.

To demonstrate responsibility, prepare for your meetings with your mentor. Prior to the meeting, you should provide a list of questions to address.

If you fail to demonstrate responsibility by being ill-prepared, your mentor could feel that his time is being wasted. You run the risk of losing your mentor's respect and commitment to mentoring.

It's important to be persistent in asking for the amount of time you need to spend with your mentor. Otherwise, your mentor may prioritize other tasks before your mentoring relationship. Remember that an effective protege is one who is responsible, dedicated, adaptable, and persistent.

Case Study: Question 1 of 2
Scenario

Dale, a training coordinator in a large health-care organization, has asked Sharon, his boss, to be his mentor. Sharon agreed to mentor Dale for a year, and she assigned him to an important project--developing a cultural diversity training initiative for all employees. Dale is meeting with Sharon to discuss the training needs analysis.

Sharon: I received your list of questions about the cultural diversity training needs analysis. Your list looks very comprehensive.

Dale: Thanks. I think I've covered all the issues, but if you should discover a missing element, please let me know.

Sharon: Will do. I should let you know that in about 20 minutes, I'm going to have to take a call from the vice president of human resources. Something has come up that must be addressed right away.

Dale: No problem, Sharon. I'll make a note of where we leave off, and we can resume next week.

Sharon: Thanks for your flexibility, Dale. You know how hectic it can be around here.

Question

What other quality did Dale display?

Options:

1. dedication
2. adaptability
3. persistence
4. credibility
5. insistence

Answer:

Option 1: This choice is incorrect. Dale did not demonstrate dedication in his meeting with Sharon. In this case, there was no opportunity to establish roles and outline the details of their mentoring relationship.

Option 2: This choice is correct. Dale demonstrated adaptability when Sharon informed him of an expected call from the vice president of human resources. He took the news with ease and displayed his ability to adapt to his mentor's needs.

Option 3: This choice is incorrect. In this case, Dale did not demonstrate persistence in asking for the amount of time he needed to spend with Sharon. He accommodated Sharon's need to attend to pressing matters.

Option 4: This option is incorrect. Credibility is a quality that a mentor, not a protege, should display.

Option 5: This choice is incorrect. Insistence is a quality that a mentor, not a protege, should display.

Case Study: Question 2 of 2

Did Dale act responsibly?

Options:

1. Yes.
2. No.

Answer:

Option 1: The answer is yes. Dale acted responsibly by sending Sharon a list of questions about the cultural diversity training needs analysis before their meeting. He prepared in advance for his meeting with Sharon.

Option 2: The answer is not no. Dale did act responsibly because he prepared in advance for his meeting with Sharon. He maximized the use of Sharon's time by sending the list of questions to her prior to the meeting.

Dale acted responsibly by preparing a list of questions about the cultural diversity training needs analysis and sending it to Sharon before the meeting. By doing so, he was prepared to make the most of the time he spent with her.

Had he not been prepared for the meeting, they would have not maximized their time together, and Dale may have left a bad impression on Sharon. Dale displayed adaptability when he graciously accepted Sharon's need to interrupt their meeting.

Had he been less flexible, Sharon may have lost enthusiasm about donating her valuable time to mentoring Dale. Enter into and maintain your mentoring relationship as an equal partner. Act in ways that prove to your mentor that you are a responsible, dedicated, adaptable, and persistent protege.

REFERENCES

References
1. **Gung Ho!** - 1997, Blanchard, Ken, and Sheldon Bowles, William Morrow & Co.
2. **Motivation and Goal Setting: How to Set and Achieve Goals and Inspire Others** - 1998, Cairo, Jim, National Press Publications, Inc.
3. **Knock Em' Dead Management: The Ultimate Guide to Managing People, Setting Goals, and Achieving Success** - 2003, Yate, Martin, and Peter Sander, Adams Media
4. **Communicating at Work** - 1993, Alessandre, T., and Phil Hunsaker, Fireside Books
5. **Surviving Job Stress** - 2002, Arden, John B., The Career Press
6. **Eliminate Stress from your Life Forever: A Simple Program for Better Living** - 2004, Atkinson, William, and Sharon Peterson

7. **Communicate with Confidence** - 1994, Booher, Dianna, McGraw-Hill
8. **Harvard Business Essentials: Hiring And Keeping The Best People** - 2002, Capelli, Peter, Harvard Business School Publishing
9. **Difficult People** - 1990, Cava, Robert, Key Porter Books,
10. **Conquer Your Stress** - 2000, Cooper, Cary L., and S. Palmer, CIPD,
11. **The 7 Habits of Highly Effective People** - 1999, Covey, S., Simon & Schuster,
12. **Speaking Your Mind in 101 Difficult Situations** - 2002, Gabor, Don, Conversation Arts Media
13. **Executive Health: How to Recognize Health Danger Signals and Manage Stress Successfully** - 1978, Goldberg, P., McGraw-Hill
14. **I'm OK, You're OK** - 1996, Harris, Thomas, Avon
15. **Reducing Stress** - 1998, Hindle, T., Dorling Kindersley,
16. **Balancing Work & Life** - 2002, Holden, R., and B. Renshaw, Dorling Kindersley,
17. **The Handbook of Coaching** - 1999, Hudson, Frederic M., Ph.D, Jossey-Bass,
18. **Psychological Stress and the Coping Process** - 1984, Lazarus, R. S, Springer,
19. **Stress, Appraisal and Coping** - 1984, Lazarus, R. S., and S. Folkman, Springer,
20. **Developing Positive Assertiveness, Third Edition** - 2002, Lloy, Sam R., Crisp Learning,

21. **You Can't Afford the Luxury of a Negative Thought: A Guide to Positive Thinking** - 2001, McWilliams, Peter, and John Roger, HarperCollins,
22. **Managing Your Career For Dummies** - 2000, Messmer, Max, Hungry Minds,
23. **Stress at Work** - 1999, NIOSH
24. **Locus of Control in Personality** - 1976, Phares, E. Jerry, General Learning,
25. **How To Make The Most Of Your Workday** - 2001, Pickering, Peg, Career Press,
26. **Encyclopaedia of Occupational Health and Safety** - 1997, Stellman J., ed., International **Labour Office, The Ultimate Career Success Workbook** - 2003, Yeung, Rob, Kogan Page,
27. **Problem-creating vs. Problem-solving** - Neenan, M., Stress News, April 1999, Occupational Stress
28. **Adult Learner at Work: The Challenges of Lifelong Education in the Millenium** - 2002, Burns, Robert, Allen & Unwin Pty., Limited
29. **Peak Learning: How to Create Your Own Lifelong Education Program for Personal Enlightenment and Professional Success** - 1999, Gross, Ronald, Jeremy P. Tarcher
30. **More Learning in Less Time: A Guide for Students, Professionals, Career-Changers, and Lifelong Learners** - 1999, Kahn, Norma B., Ways-To Books

31. **Building a Career Development Program -** 1996, Knowdell, Richard L., Davies-Black Publishing
32. **Lifelong Learning in Action -** 2003, Longworth, Norman, Kagan Page
33. **Success Skills: Strategies for Study and Lifelong Learning -** 2001, Marks-Beale, Abby, South-Western Educational Pub.
34. **Coaching and Mentoring -** 2000, Parsloe, Eric, and Monika Wray, Kogan Page
35. **Successful Lifelong Learning: Ten Tactics for Today and Tomorrow -** 2000, Steinbach, Robert, Crisp Learning,
36. **The Mentoring Manual -** 2000, Whittaker, Mike, and Ann Cartwright, Gower Publishing

GLOSSARY

Glossary
A
Achievable goal - A goal that is articulated in a way that clearly defines the objective, standards, and conditions for success.

Alternative goal - A method for achieving a portion of a goal that has proven to be too aggressive or too challenging to be immediately attainable.

C
Conditions component - A phrase in a statement of a goal that places limits on acceptable activities or results that result from efforts to attain the goal.

D
Development goal - A goal that describes plans to acquire new abilities or to enhance existing abilities.

H
High-risk goal - High-risk goals often require a large investment of time and effort. Failure to achieve a high-risk goal results in a substantial loss of invested resources.

L

Low-risk goal - Low-risk goals usually require a small investment of time and effort. Failure to achieve a low-risk goal costs a goal seeker little in the way of lost resources.

O

Objective component - A phrase in a description of a goal that defines the activities that will be performed or the outcomes that will be sought to attain the goal.

P

Performance goal - A goal that sets standards for results you want to achieve in your regular activities. These goals usually set targets that challenge your existing abilities.

Personal importance - The degree to which a goal satisfies your personal needs or values.

Priorities matrix - A method for plotting data points that represent the importance and availability of resources of a group of goals. The position of data points on the matrix indicates the relative priority of goals.

Professional importance - The degree to which your goals satisfy your employer's needs or values.

R

Resource readiness - The ease with which the resources you need to achieve a goal can be accessed and used.

Resource urgency - The time pressure to use available resources needed to achieve a goal before they become available.

S

Standards component - A standards component describes a measurement to determine whether an objective has been reached. Common types of standards include counting successful results, measuring the degree of change, or setting a deadline for completion.

www.ingramcontent.com/pod-product-compliance
Lightning Source LLC
Chambersburg PA
CBHW020903180526
45163CB00007B/2609